JAPAN UNESCORTED

A PRACTICAL GUIDE TO DISCOVERING JAPAN ON YOUR OWN

by

JAMES K. WEATHERLY

Published by
JAPAN AIR LINES CO., LTD.

Printed in Japan by KOSSAI SHUPPANSHA

CONTENTS

Why This Book? 4
What You're Up Against 5
How to Cope 7
Japan Now 8
How Japan Got This Way 9
Mattress for the Night 11
Eating the Japanese Way 17
City to City 19
Meeting the Japanese 22
When to Visit Japan 23
Useful Tips 24
Japan Arrival 25
Prices 25
Tokyo: Throbbing Nerve Center 26
    Getting Your Bearings 27
    Ginza-Nihombashi 35
    Asakusa 45
    Shinjuku 49
    Ueno-Nippori 53
    Harajuku-Omotesando 59
    Roppongi 63
    Akasaka 64
    Shopping Off the Tourist Trail 66
    Museums for the Specialist 67
    Tokyo Day Trips 68
Kyoto: Traditional Japanese Taste 74
    Higashiyama 75
    Kiyomizu-Gion 79
    Arashiyama 80
    Zen Gardens, Palaces 81
    Nara, Uji, Ohara & Mt. Hiei 86
Himeji: Idyllic Castle 91
Kurashiki: Godown Galleries 93
Nagoya: Shrines and Cormorants 98
Takayama: Life in the Mountains 103
Kanazawa: Classy Castle Town 112
Sendai: Northern Gateway 120
Nagasaki: Peephole to Outside 134
Sapporo: Oriental Kansas City 141
Bibliography 152

WHY THIS BOOK?

The visitor to Japan has traditionally been coddled by Japanese tour operators from the moment he/she sets foot on Japanese soil until his/her departure. These operators are still there, of course, and as willing to coddle as ever. But such coddling is expensive anywhere in the world, and generally more so in Japan. For that reason the members of the Japanese travel industry — hotels, restaurants, sightseeing tour companies — who have catered to the Japanese traveler on a tight budget for many years have recently begun to realize that some foreign sojourners would rather travel the way the Japanese do and are starting to throw open their doors to visitors from abroad, albeit not very widely.

Companies like Japan Air Lines which are more closely in touch with foreign travelers have helped get the doors ajar. All that's necessary to widen the crack is for the visitor to put his big foot in. For the Japanese travel industry, the attitude about the individual traveler from overseas is "wait and see".

The industry's eyes are on you, dear vagabond on your own. This book was designed to help you get your foot in the door, and more, to know how to conduct yourself once inside. No attempt was made to cover every nook and cranny of the country. Some of the weightier volumes in the Bibliography are more comprehensive. Rather, "Japan Unescorted" was designed to put you on the track to locations where you'll gain an understanding of Japanese life as it was — and is.

4

WHAT YOU'RE UP AGAINST

The paradox for the body on his/her own in Nippon is that while there is no country in Asia or perhaps the world more accessible by public transportation, perhaps no country is more difficult to travel in without a guide. The problem is primarily the language barrier and a general lack of experience among Japanese with people other than their own.

Another paradox: If Japanese today study English for an average of six years, why can't more people speak it? It's a question the Ministry of Education is asking, too. But the problem is far from being solved. For starters, the Japanese language — except for the great number of English words which are today used, but pronounced with Japanese phonetic sounds — is in no way like English. It grew out of the needs of a very homogeneous people packed together for many centuries on a group of islands far from the rest of the world. Living so close together the Japanese created a language that, above all else, was designed to promote harmonious relations between people.

Honorifics abound, and an indication of a man's good breeding is to be able to hide his true feelings for the sake of making the other party feel good. One party strokes with a few carefully chosen words, and the other party strokes right back.

The true meaning of what has been said, however, is often not clear. Did he mean that? Or that? You can only really know by playing the same kind of word games from an early age, which is an opportunity few foreigners have.

And still another paradox: In this world full of Sonys, Datsuns and Toyotas where the Japanese have seemingly sold something to even the African bushman, why don't they feel more comfortable with foreigners?

The answer perhaps is because their experience with non-Japanese has largely been on a business level only. This is not the same as swapping stories about the office idiot, the great weekend they had with the family in the country or their favorite baseball team.

More and more Japanese are traveling abroad and a greater number than ever are being posted to New York or Dusseldorf or Bangkok on overseas assignments. Their experiences with foreigners are beginning to penetrate the Japanese population at large, but slowly.

Deeply ingrained into the Japanese psyche is the notion

that they are very different from any other people in the world. Traditionally a division has always been made between what's "ours" and what's "theirs". Japanese things are separated from western things in the department stores. Rarely does a restaurant serving western food also serve Japanese food.

Among today's Japanese the dichotomy between East and West is less and less clear cut. They may have dinner in a French restaurant, see a Japanese translation of Shakespeare's "Romeo and Juliet" on stage, then go home and throw out their *futon* sleeping mattress on the *tatami* floor. If all this seems a little incongruous to us, it doesn't strike the Japanese that way.

Flirting with western food and fashion is one thing, but coming face to face with a real, live foreigner or, worse, having to say something in comprehensible English, is something else entirely.

The Japanese call it *gaijin shokku* or outsider shock, and the reaction can range from embarrassed giggles to hysterics. Fortunately, the former is far more common. In Tokyo, Kyoto and Osaka where foreigners are not quite such an unusual sight, there is general indifference or, at the most, a restrained curiosity. Deep in the country you may be followed for what seems like hours by wide-eyed kids. Be understanding. If a Japanese suddenly showed up on the streets of Possumtrot, Arkansas, the locals would stare too.

By no means should this speechless awe of you be taken as disrespect. The average Japanese have envied the West's technological ability from the time it was introduced. The admiration has extended to the people who created that technology as well. Having now leapt into the sphere of the superpowers, Japan is less in awe. But the memories linger.

6

The problem remains that few Japanese have had any real experience with a foreigner over an extended period of time. The traveler on his own in Japan can't change this situation overnight. But it's a step in the right direction.

HOW TO COPE

If you're traveling alone in Japan, the easiest way to surmount the language problem and the general Japanese inexperience with westerners is to get yourself a Japanese friend who can speak English. Since that could take almost as much time as learning the language, however, more practical advice is in order.

The JAL Jet Age Language Course in Japanese is available in North America. English-Japanese phrase books also offer some help, provided the user can simulate Japanese pronunciation, which is not difficult. JAL's "Speak a Little Japanese" is available from their sales offices overseas, or you can pick up one of several other phrase books at English language book stores in major Japanese cities.

In most situations you'll have to rely on English to get you through, however. Here a few hints are in order. Speak slowly, using the simplest vocabulary possible. Don't use slang and colloquialisms. Since Japanese words often end in vowel sounds, English words which end in a consonant are frequently given a vowel, usually "o" or "u", at the end.

The word "beer", for example, becomes *"biiru"* in Japanese pronunciation. The letter "l" sounds like "r" to Japanese, so any word with the letter "l" in it will be pronounced with a slight "r" sound. Hotel thus becomes *"hoteru"*.

Should the spoken word prove absolutely impossible, write out your question. Japanese generally understand written English far better than spoken, because it is written English that is emphasized in school.

If you find yourself in desperation outside Tokyo and Kyoto, you can take advantage of the Japan National Tourist Organization's (JNTO) "Travel-Phone" service. Just insert a ¥10 coin in any yellow or blue public telephone, dial 106 and tell the operator, "Collect call, TIC" (Travel Information Center). You will be connected to a Center in Tokyo or Kyoto where an English-speaking staff will be on hand to help you. The ¥10 coin will be returned on completion of the call. This service is available daily between 9 a.m.-5 p.m. In Tokyo or Kyoto dial TIC's local number as listed under these city's headings in this book.

JAPAN NOW

For most westerners, the lure of Japan began with some outdated travel posters of young girls in kimono gazing at Mt. Fuji. The fear of the educated westerner is that neither the kimono — nor Mt. Fuji — is visible anymore. Fear not. Both are still very much on the scene, though the kimono-wearer is today usually a grandma; and Mt. Fuji's visibility from the Tokyo metropolis depends, as it always has, on the weather (more often visible from October through February).

Perhaps the most interesting thing about the Japan experience for the foreigner, though, is to observe a society that has moved so rapidly into the 20th century, while at the same time been able to hang on to its traditional set of values. Sincerity, honesty, dedication to hard work, a constant striving for doing even the tiniest job well, a willingness to sacrifice individual will for the good of the community — these are the basic beliefs that have kept and to a large extent are still keeping the Japanese society together. It's the American Protestant ethic, without the religious overtones. And in a land where less than 1 per cent are Christians!

One of the joys of traveling in Japan is seeing these common beliefs being put into practice. Whether it's the little old lady or man who cleans the public toilet, or the giant, trading company president — whatever the task at hand — it's done with the enthusiasm of a zealot. Probe deeper, however, and you'll discover few Japanese sit down and analyze exactly why they are running, or in which direction. They have so far been spared the American pastime of self-analysis. When a decision must be made as to whether they will do what they really want to do, or do what their family, company or the society at large expects, it's the group and not the individual that usually wins.

Little signs are up everywhere among the young people that the perennial self-sacrifice is now being questioned. Privately the young generation will frankly admit that they'd like a life of their own outside the group. Young couples now generally live separately from their parents.

More young men are forsaking the company of their male colleagues in the office after working hours to be with their wives and children. A few dream of "dropping out" of the proverbial rat race to raise vegetables in the country. There are even a few willing to forsake their homeland altogether for space and more freedom to "do their own thing" in another land.

Attachment to family holds strong, and this will not quickly change, given the potent symbiosis between mother and child. A Japanese mother is expected by her husband, the family and society to completely devote herself to the little darlings, regardless of her natural inclinations. Even the least observant visitor can't help but notice how Japanese mothers, and often fathers as well, cluck and coo over everything a child does. The dependence created by that kind of smothering relationship is never completely broken.

For the western visitor all this togetherness is astounding, a harking back to simpler times in our own societies when a sense of community was still a strong force. You'll be asking yourself over and over again how the Japanese have been able to preserve this sense under living conditions in many ways more chaotic than our own. If you arrive at any answers, your trip to Japan will have been worth every minute. As a lone wanderer you have an opportunity to discover what makes Japan Japanese — their unique way of seeing and doing things that makes a visit to this country so special.

HOW JAPAN GOT THIS WAY

The miracle of today's Japan didn't just happen, of course. The energy which zoomed the Japanese economic state into the number two position behind the United States after World War II has naturally been at work for a long time before, expressing itself sometimes peacefully, often not.

At no time in their history have the Japanese just sat

around contemplating the universe, for they are by nature a restless people given to doing more than thinking. Their history teaches that they are above all, practical. When a conflict arises, they jump to the fore, driven more by gut reaction to the issues than by reasoning. Not being philosophically bent, they spend little time looking for the principles involved.

During the past century since western ideas came into vogue, the nation has often been busy showing the rest of the world that it can compete equally as well, if not better, whether it be conquering other nations such as the major world powers were doing through World War II, or building better automobiles.

Prior to the Meiji period (1868–1912), however, the power struggles were confined primarily to Japanese shores. Much of the nation's history before the Tokugawa (Edo) period (1603–1867), named after the family of military *shoguns* who took control of the nation after it had been unified at the beginning of the 17th century, centered on feuds between local lords or between militant Buddhist sects.

SHOGUN

Until after World War II, the Japanese Emperor was revered as god, but outside of his duties as spiritual leader, he seldom held much power. Throughout recorded history the Emperor or Empress were constantly being manipulated by power-hungry families, first by regents within the Imperial Court, later by military dictators. Even when the Emperor Meiji was restored to power in 1868, the event was less an achievement for the Emperor than for an able body of feudal clan leaders who simply used him for their own purposes.

Foreign influence has washed over the country in waves, first from China — often through Korea — and much more recently from western nations. In contrast to the Chinese, who traditionally followed their own ways and rejected the ways of others, the Japanese saw nothing wrong in discarding their methods when they thought the foreign method was better. But whatever was borrowed from other cultures was eventually tailored specifically to meet Japanese needs.

With the Meiji Restoration came Japan's craving for things western. For education, they patterned their system after that of the European continent. The Japanese army was modeled on Germany's, the Navy on England's. During the American postwar occupation, it was America's turn. The Japanese Constitution was rewritten following American lines and thought processes. For the first time the Japanese were given individual freedoms, although the average Japanese did not know quite what to do with them. The concept is just now beginning to be understood. No one is quite sure where this new wave of influence will lead.

The modern craving for things western stems partly at least from the nearly 250 years of enforced isolation by the Tokugawa *Shoguns*. Except for the port of Nagasaki where the Dutch were allowed to trade, the nation was sealed off like a sarcophagus from the rest of the world. Guided by neo-Confucian ethics, the Tokugawas divided the society into four classes: military, farmers, craftsmen and merchants in that order. Each class's life was prescribed, right down to the type of clothes its members could wear. But during the long period of peace it proved an impossible task to keep the classes in line. With no battles to fight, the military gradually gave themselves up to sensual pleasures. Not content at the bottom of the social scale, the merchants saw their chance and eventually took the reins. For the first time in Japanese history the common people found ways to gain first wealth and then power. The great cities of Edo (Tokyo) and Osaka flowered, their attractions well documented in the woodblock prints familiar to westerners.

MATTRESS FOR THE NIGHT

Since this book is geared for the traveler on his/her own and probably on a limited budget, only a few of many hotel possibilities in Japan will be explained — the business hotels in the cities, *minshuku*, or family inns, pensions and publicly-owned lodgings usually located in the country or away from central business districts.

Business hotels, a rather recent phenomenon, are designed for the traveling businessman less interested in frills than a place to wash and a clean bed. They are most often "western style", meaning you sleep in a bed rather than on a *futon* (mattress) on the *tatami* floor, and the toilet will be designed for sitting rather than squatting. Both room and bath are miniscule, but often bright and cheery. There are usually no restaurants in the hotel, but it is always located in a business area where a restaurant is never far away. Of course, these establishments offer privacy that is nonexistent at the *minshuku*. Rates average ¥4,800 per night for a single.

Recommended business hotels will be listed under the various cities in this book. JAL, the Japan National Tourist Organization (JNTO) or your travel agent can provide the names as well. Travelers already in Japan can make reservations at travel agencies or directly with the hotels by telephone. Unlike *minshuku,* the business hotels are likely to have a staff on hand who can handle enough English to take your reservation.

Minshuku are for the independent traveler who wants to go native as much as possible and be in an atmosphere conducive to meeting Japanese. They are almost always owned by a family, so it's more like being a guest in a private home. This is an appealing prospect for the traveler who wants to get to know the people. But be warned, few *minshuku* owners can speak more than the bare minimum of English. Again, an understanding attitude works wonders. Some foreign guests leave raving about the experience, even though they were able to communicate only with grunts and gestures.

The *minshuku* range from charming, old farm houses with an *irori* (fireplace) built into the *tatami* floor, exposed beams, sliding paper doors and thatched roofs to new, multistory structures whose exteriors are modern and interiors are plastic and cardboard.

Depending on the place, you may have a room to yourself or share it with others, the latter being a good possibility during the busy summer months. In either case, the toilet, bathing and dining facilities will be communal.

By the time you've reached a *minshuku* on your own, you'll no doubt have had some experience with Japanese toilets. The chief difference from the ones we use at home is that they are built flush with the floor, and there are no seats. If this crouching in a fetal position sounds like an impossible feat, remember that far more of the world's people squat than sit, and doctors insist the position is "natural".

One of the chief attractions of the toilet at a *minshuku* is that it's probably the only place you'll have a chance to be alone. Each is in its own individual stall, usually with a lock on the door. Locked or not, however, someone will probably give two taps on the door to make sure it's occupied. The custom is to give two taps right back — and you'd best follow the rule or the person outside will tap to eternity.

These toilets are usually shared by both men and women, and the men at the urinals are supposed to be ignored. The Japanese have learned to pretend anything offensive, especially bodily functions, is not there.

Then there is the plastic slipper syndrome. The reasoning is that the toilet is, after all, a dirty place. The slippers you put on at the inn's entrance for wearing in the halls, therefore, just won't do in the toilet. So plastic slippers always await you at the door, and in some places there will be yet another pair waiting outside the toilet stall. All this fussing with slippers is questionable from a sanitary standpoint, but it's good exercise.

The *ofuro* (bath) is also shared by both sexes at these places — but almost always separately. If you're not quite sure whether yours or the other sex is inside, take a look at the clothes lying in the plastic baskets in the dressing area before entering. In this uni-sex age, however, such examinations are not always foolproof.

OFURO

The *minshuku* guest always carries a small hand towel and soap in his/her kit, as they are seldom provided. Once inside the bath itself, you'll spy a wall of water taps situated at about mid-calf level and a cauldron of boiling water, usually set into the floor. Grab a miniature plastic stool and a pail and position yourself in front of a pair of water taps — one for hot and one for cold running water. If you can't find any hot water tap, it means you'll have to dip the hot water from the tub and temper it with the cold running water. All soaping is done outside the tub. As you'll quickly discover, the Japanese can spend hours gouging at every crevice with a variety of devices to get the dirt and old skin off. This is as much a ritual as a means of getting clean. No foreigner can match them for time consumed in scrubbing without losing his/her epidermis. The soap is carefully rinsed off by pouring buckets of fresh water over yourself.

Then it's soaking time in the cauldron. The water temperature can range from tepid to torrid, so beware. If it's too hot, it's quite acceptable to add some cold water. Not all Japanese are fond of being boiled alive either. When you think it's bearable, don't be finicky. Get yourself submerged as quickly as possible. Within minutes the cares of the day will quickly pass, and you'll discover why these few minutes in the water before bed are to the Japanese a natural birthright. It's such a pleasure, many can't wait until before bedtime and have one bath before dinner too. At some *minshuku*, however, you'll be told when to take your bath. Remember not to pull the plug — everyone uses the same water.

You'll spring out of the tub with your skin a rosy red and the steam rising off your body. Better take it easy for a few minutes until you regain your senses. You can dry yourself with the same hand towel you used for washing by constantly wringing out the excess water, or you can carry a bath towel, as many Japanese now do.

The price at a *minshuku* includes two meals — dinner and breakfast — which are usually served family-style in one of the large rooms on the main floor of the building. You'll sit on the floor before a low table. Most of the dishes will be spread out before you in a vast array, and no attempt is made at serving in courses. Japanese take no concern about hot dishes being hot and cold dishes being cold. The only things you can depend on being hot are the soy bean soup, rice and green tea. Beer and sake are always available. But you'll be charged extra for these.

The food usually consists of a variety of local delicacies — ocean fish and shell fish, if you're near the sea; mountain trout and vegetables in the mountain areas, and the inevitable pickled cabbage, turnips or radishes which you flavor with soy sauce. This is a garnish to the generally bland and tasteless sticky rice.

The foreigner who must have his coffee in the morning and wants his eggs done to a turn with bacon on the side will have a problem in a *minshuku*. Except in rare cases where the host or hostess is willing to make special concessions (and this is always trouble for them), you'll have to be content with a piece of salted fish, more soy bean soup and rice.

The morning custom is to plop a raw egg over the steaming rice in your bowl, stir it up with your chopsticks, add a little soy sauce to taste, then after dipping a thin slice of dried seaweed into your soy sauce, you wrap the seaweed around a bite-size ball of egg and rice with your chopsticks and plunge it into your mouth. The swallowing is sometimes difficult. Forget the taste and think of all that nutrition.

Bedding down in a *minshuku* is also in the traditional Japanese way. You spread a mattress (two, if you like your bed soft) from the closet out on the *tatami* floor, tuck the clean sheet provided around it, throw over the lighter *futon* quilt (usually no top sheet), place that small pillow, presumably filled with steel balls (actually buckwheat chaff), at the head — and you're ready to crawl in for a good night's rest. Remember to put your bedding back in the closet in the morning.

Minshuku guests are reminded that in a land where practically every service is provided, the *minshuku* is not a service establishment. You do practically everything by yourself, except make your own food. When not pressed for time, the owners can be expected to be very helpful in offering tips on what to see in the area, but the generally low rates do not allow for paid help to meet your every whim. This should be no sacrifice to the traveler alone in Japan.

JAL, JNTO and major travel agents can give you the names and addresses of *minshuku* in the areas you plan to visit. If the *minshuku* you select is a member of the Japan Minshuku Association and you want to make reservations in advance, write to the **Japan Minshuku Association,** 2-10-8 Hyakunin-cho, Shinjuku-ku, Tokyo 161. Send your reservations request at least one month in advance of the date of your stay. If available, you'll need to send a deposit by International Postal Money Order at least three weeks in advance (¥1,000 per night per person). Be sure and include a "Coupon Response International" from your local post office to cover the postage. *Minshuku* reservations can be made on the spot in Tokyo at the organization's **Japan Minshuku Center** in the basement of the Kotsu Kaikan Bldg. on the east side of Yurakucho Station (Tel. 216-6556). *Minshuku* prices are usually ¥4,000 per person per night, including dinner and breakfast. In Kyoto and Nara, breakfast only. ¥5,500-¥6,000 with two meals in the Hakone resort area. Children 4-11 get a ¥300 discount.

FUTON

Similar in style to the *minshuku,* except they are usually government-run, are the **Kokumin Shukusha,** or public lodgings in scenic spots or national parks (average ¥4,000 per person per night, with two meals). There are also the **Kokumin Kyuka Mura,** or vacation villages with recreational facilities included (¥4,500-¥6,900 per person per night with two meals). Write to the **Kokumin Kyuka Mura Service Center** for reservations at Tokyo Kotsu

Kaikan, 2-10-1 Yurakucho, Chiyoda-ku, Tokyo (Tel. 216-2085). Reservations for either of these types of accommodations should be made at least six months in advance, as they are popular.

Also located in resort areas and especially the ski areas are **pensions**, where prices are a bit higher (¥6,000-¥7,000 per person with two meals), but facilities are usually better. Like *minshuku,* the pensions are owned by families, often young couples who fled the big cities for the great outdoors. Reservations can be made through travel agents or the **Pension Reservations Center**, Inuzuka Bldg., second floor, 2-4-11 Sarugakucho, Chiyoda-ku, Tokyo (Tel. 295-6333).

Rock-bottom prices are offered by **Japan Youth Hostels, Inc. (JYH)**, a private company operating almost 500 hostels throughout the country, and the more than 75 hostels operated by the national or regional governments. Rates average about ¥1,800 per night for a bed only, the government-operated spots being cheaper. Meals cost from ¥400 to ¥650, or you can cook for yourself in the central kitchen facilities. These are essentially dormitory operations, with strict check-in (between 3 and 8 p.m.) and check-out (not later than 10 a.m.) times (closed between 10 a.m. and 3 p.m.). Curfew time is 9 p.m. Lights out at 10 p.m., which may be a bit early in Tokyo.

If JYH appeals to you and your first stop is Tokyo, visit their office at the Hoken Kaikan Bldg., second floor, 1-2 Sadohara-cho, Ichigaya, Shinjuku-ku, Tokyo 162 (269-5831/3), a five-minute walk from the JNR Ichigaya Station (Sobu Line). If you're not already a member of the International Youth Hostel Federation, you can buy an International Guest Card here (¥3,000, bring a passport-type photo) as well as pick up copies of the JYH Handbook with handy maps of the hostels and their English-language pamphlet for foreign visitors (the latter also available at JNTO's Tokyo and Kyoto Tourist Information Centers (TIC).

EATING THE JAPANESE WAY

Japanese food offers infinitely more taste possibilities than the *tempura* and *sukiyaki* foreigners know. The emphasis is on enhancing the natural taste rather than camouflaging it. Rice is the staple, boiled until sticky and not until dry, and, indeed, the word for meal in Japanese (*gohan*), means rice.

Meats are chopped into bite-size pieces that can easily be picked up with your chopsticks. They are never overcooked, often raw (including paper-thin slices of chicken, beef or wild game, besides the more famous raw fish). These are most often dipped into a tiny dish of sauce, usually with a soy sauce base and a few fresh ingredients such as ginger, onions or grated radish.

Vegetables range from all the familiar things such as carrots and cucumbers to wild mountain roots and grasses that may be served fresh, boiled, pickled or deep-fried.

All meals will be accompanied with a bowl of hot soup, either made from soy-bean paste or a clear fish stock, and a pickled garnish of cucumbers, cabbage, radishes, etc. The pickles are usually eaten with the rice at the end of the meal.

Like so many things Japanese, the food is subtle. At first it is seemingly tasteless. Bite-by-bite, it grows on you, and in time you start believing that little twig, root or flower really did taste a bit different than the one you had during the last meal. But this takes time.

Regardless of what you think about the taste, you will inevitably be intrigued with the way it's served. With no attempt to match colors or sizes, plates and bowls are selected to suit the food's color and texture, often with only a few morsels in a sizeable dish.

Many westerners will probably pale at the thought of rice, noodles and a bit of fish everyday. For that reason some foreign restaurants where the taste is close to authentic will be recommended under the restaurant listings in cities where available.

CITY TO CITY

The traveler will depend for the most part on the country's extensive railroad network, principally the Japan National Railways (JNR), and the private railways which supplement it.

Except for the "**Condensed Railway Timetable**" (available from JNTO), however, there are no JNR schedules in English. The tourist heading for remote areas had better get the details about trains between the cities and towns he's visiting from an English-speaking Japanese before he leaves the big city. English-speaking staff are rare indeed at JNR stations, except at the **Tokyo Station Travel Service Center**, but the man at the ticket window will surely understand the name of your destination and how many tickets you want. So far so good.

Now the problem arises. What type of train will you use? There is the **local** (*futsu*) which misses not a single whistle-stop, but requires no extra-charge tickets. Then there's the **express** (*kyuko*) which stops only at major stations and requires an extra-charge ticket (*kyuko-ken*). Finally, there's the **limited express** (*tokkyu*) which also requires an extra-charge ticket (*tokkyu-ken*). All usually have first class Green Cars where you get a white linen cover over the back of the seat and a chance to maintain your peace-of-mind — for an extra price. The *tokkyu* and *kyuko* have reserved seats only at a small extra charge. Reservations can be made one month in advance at JNR stations or through travel agents.

The foreign visitor planning to stay in Japan at least a week can save himself both a lot of time in figuring out the complicated system and money by purchasing a **Japan Rail Pass** good for seven, 14 or 21 days at JAL offices or from authorized travel agents outside Japan. Both "Ordinary" and "Green" passes are available, the latter entitling the holder to a seat in the Green Car. Seven-day "Ordinary" Passes cost ¥21,000 — ¥30,000 for the "Green" Passes; 14-day "Ordinary" at ¥33,000 — ¥48,000 for the "Green" Passes; and 21-day "Ordinary" at ¥44,000 — ¥64,000 for the "Green" Passes.

The JAL office or travel agent will issue after full payment a JALMCO which you exchange for the actual Pass either at the JNR Information and Ticket Office at the New Tokyo International Airport, Narita or at one of 12 JNR Travel Service Centers. Japan Rail Passes can't be purchased in Japan. The passes can be used on any of JNR's

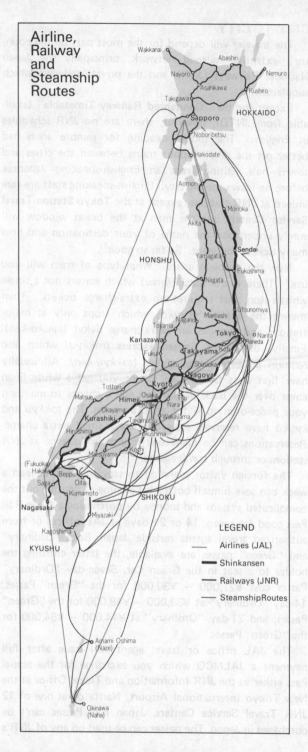

Airline, Railway and Steamship Routes

Wakkanai
Abashiri
Nayoro
Nemuro
Asahikawa
Kushiro
Takigawa
HOKKAIDO
Sapporo
Noboribetsu
Hakodate
Aomori
Morioka
Akita
Sendai
Yamagata
Fukushima
Niigata
HONSHU
Nagano
Utsunomiya
Toyama
Maebashi
Kanazawa
Takayama
Tokyo
Narita
Fukui
Kofu
Haneda
Gifu
Shizuoka
Nagoya
Tsu
Kyoto
Tottori
Osaka
Nara
Himeji
Kobe
Wakayama
Matsue
Okayama
Kurashiki
Takamatsu
Hiroshima
Tokushima
Matsuyama
Kochi
SHIKOKU
(Fukuoka)
Hakata
Beppu
Saga
Oita
Kumamoto
Nagasaki
Miyazaki
Kagoshima
KYUSHU

LEGEND
— Airlines (JAL)
━ Shinkansen
— Railways (JNR)
— Steamship Routes

Amami Oshima
(Naze)

Okinawa
(Naha)

20

trains, buses or ferryboats. Sleeping accommodations, however, are at the regular fares.

Japan's famous **Bullet Trains** (*Shinkansen*) need no explanation. They are reputedly still the world's fastest, making the country's rugged terrain seem superfluous to get around, over and — by tunnel — through. Fares are naturally higher than on the regular lines (Tokyo-Fukuoka (Hakata) one way fare, for example, is ¥18,400). But you must also consider the time saved. The regular seven or eight-hour trip to Kyoto by train takes less than three hours by *Shinkansen*.

There are two types of *Shinkansen* — the *Hikari* which stops only at major stations, and the *Kodama* which stops at more stations, but is still much faster than the regular trains. Only the first four cars of the *Kodama* have reserved seats. Most seats are reserved on the *Hikari*.

Individual JAL passengers can make *Shinkansen* reservations before leaving home through JAL's computerized reservations system. After confirmation, a Seat Reservation Slip is issued through the JAL office. On arrival in Japan the Slip is exchanged for the real ticket at any of JNR's Travel Service Centers at Narita (New Tokyo International Airport), Tokyo, Yokohama, Kyoto, Osaka or Hiroshima. Reservations can be made from three to 60 days prior to actual departure time of the train in Japan.

Train passengers are reminded to hang on to all of their tickets throughout their journey. The tickets will be collected when you exit at your final destination.

Japan's private railways are often convenient in and around the big cities and in resort areas, and usually cheaper than JNR. Certain lines will be recommended under destination headings.

JNR also operates "Highway Buses" between major cities such as Tokyo, Nagoya, Kyoto and Osaka at fares lower than their trains. Special non-stop "Dream" buses depart Tokyo Station every night for Nagoya (¥5,500), Kyoto (¥7,100) and Osaka (¥7,450), arriving the following morning. (Nightly departures also from Osaka, Kyoto and Nagoya to Tokyo). All seats are reserved, and reservations should be made well in advance.

In really remote areas of Japan local buses reach spots the train won't. Departures are usually scheduled for easy connections from railways. Fare payment varies on these buses, but the usual system is to collect a tab on entry which shows the zone where you boarded. When you exit, you match the zone number on your tab with that on the fare board at the front of the bus and read the corresponding fare. On some buses there is a conductor who collects fares while roaming up and down the aisle. You simply tell your destination and the conductor will tell you the fare.

Finally, you might consider one of the **inter-coastal steamships** which, of course, take longer than the train, but offer more scenic possibilities, especially through the Inland Sea between Osaka or Kobe to Beppu (Kyushu). This overnight trip offered by Kansai Steamship Co. takes 14 hours from Osaka, with fares from ¥5,700.

From Tokyo and nearby Kawasaki there are inexpensive car ferries to ports on other islands — time consuming, but cheap (Tokyo-Tomakomai (Hokkaido)—¥11,500; Tokyo-Tokushima (Shikoku) — ¥8,200; Kawasaki-Hyuga (near Miyazaki, Kyushu) — ¥16,200).

MEETING THE JAPANESE

This is a formal society. No one walks up, grabs your hand and says, "Hello. My name's Yukio. What's yours?" The Japanese prefer introductions through others. So the wise traveler who really wants to meet Japanese had better lay the ground work well before his/her departure from home.

If you know a Japanese, show your interest and explain that you're going to Japan. The chances are good the Japanese will make an effort to put you in touch with friends or relatives on your arrival.

The foreigner on the street in Japan generally attracts only the Japanese eager to speak English. The rest are perhaps curious, but too shy to initiate a conversation. Being thought of as an instant English-speaking machine is not especially flattering. But never mind. If you have anything in common after the English break, let it develop.

There are organizations in Tokyo geared especially to bring the foreigner and the Japanese together. Again, the prime motivation for the Japanese is English conversation. But it's a start. The **Japan International Friendship Center,** 7-2 Shinanomachi, Shinjuku-ku, Tokyo 160 (tel. 341-9064 in the afternoon), also known as the International 3F Club, sponsors classes in traditional Japanese arts and outings both in and out of the city for a small fee.

Teijin Educational System Co., Ltd. (TESCO), 1-1-1 Minami-Aoyama, Minato-ku, Tokyo 107 (Tel. 404-7003) offers similar activities and can also put you in touch with a Japanese as a sightseeing or shopping guide. They also have a home visit program (call Ms. Akimoto, Tel. 478-6577.).

A final possibility is to take advantage of the "**Home Visit System**" under sponsorship of JNTO and the governments of Tokyo, Yokohama, Nagoya, Otsu, Osaka, Kyoto, Kobe and Kagoshima. By applying to either the JNTO Tourist Information Centers in Tokyo or Kyoto or the government offices in the other cities, foreign visitors can arrange to visit a Japanese family in their home for an hour. The JNTO and city offices are closed on Saturday afternoons and on Sundays and holidays. Allow at least a day to make the arrangements. JNTO publishes a Home Visit System brochure listing the offices where you can apply and explaining what you can expect from the experience.

As is true anywhere, a real friend is often better discovered by chance than calculation. As a traveler alone, your chances for contact are far better than the person following the well-trodden tourist trail.

WHEN TO VISIT JAPAN

There are two major considerations. One is the weather. The other, trying to travel when the Japanese don't. Japan has four distinct seasons with a climate not unlike that of the U.S. Mid-Atlantic states. Winters are cool, but bright and sunny, along the Pacific Coast; frigid and usually snow-covered along the Japan Sea and on Hokkaido Island. Spring is mild and the cherry trees in full bloom are not a myth, but you can expect rain and mist along with the flowers. June is the so-called "rainy" month, but you can easily see more rain in April or May. July and August are hotter than on the equator, with humidity matching that of a South American jungle. Wear as little as possible and carry a big fan. Fall is easily the most reliable season for bright, blue skies, plus the lure of the fall foliage which starts in Hokkaido from late September and moves down the archipelago reaching Tokyo and Kyoto in early November and southern Kyushu a bit later.

During Japanese holidays, and especially the holidays which follow each other consecutively, be prepared for all public transportation to be packed to the ceilings and windows — literally. The New Year's holidays begin a few days before January 1 and continue throughout the first week in the year. During this period and again in late July or early August the big city dwellers return to their home villages in the country en masse, making a last-minute reserved seat on anything virtually impossible.

Another period to be avoided at all costs is "Golden Week", which begins with the Emperor's Birthday on April 29 and continues through Children's Day on May 5. This is the time for many Japanese to discover their own country, or for some to take trips overseas. It's virtually impossible again to get a reserved seat or a hotel room unless you plan well ahead. School vacation begins in mid-July and continues through August. While perhaps not quite as crowded as the periods mentioned above, these two months are still the favorite for Japanese travelers, and especially those with families. If you're coming to Japan at that time, again, plan and make reservations well in advance.

While the Japanese are roaming the countryside, however, their big cities are relatively quiet and empty. Japanese vacation periods are generally good times for a foreigner to discover Tokyo under less crowded conditions.

USEFUL TIPS

The following will add to your comfort or pleasure, maybe save you embarrassment:

Carry pocket-size tissue, because public rest rooms rarely provide toilet paper; a **handkerchief** to dry your hands in these places, because paper towels are a relatively unknown commodity; a **can opener** and **bottle opener**, if you're expecting to picnic; a **small flashlight**, for a better look at works of art that are often displayed in near or total darkness.

Wear soft-soled shoes, and preferably loafers or slip-ons. The gravel and stone paths of the temples and shrines and public parks are murder on a good pair of shoes and your feet, though Japan's fashion-conscious young ladies sprint over them in spike heels.

Slip-ons are the most practical, because you'll be constantly taking your shoes off and putting them on when entering *minshuku*, temples, homes, sometimes even museums and shops. Don't forget that taking your shoes off is a hard and fast rule when you are entering a *tatami* room. The number of places you'll be forsaking shoes for plastic slippers will amaze you. Plan accordingly.

Don't tip. Foreign visitors from countries where tipping is an established custom find it hard to break the habit. Some taxi drivers and restaurant and hotel personnel may accept a tip, often because they don't know how to refuse in English. But no one expects it, and more often it creates embarrassment. Small gifts in return for some kindness are something else. They are appreciated, often cherished. Any sort of trinket or doll from your own hometown, something typical of the area from which you come, is best.

JAPAN ARRIVAL

Practically all JAL International flights from North America and Europe land at the New Tokyo International Airport, Narita, a distance of 66 kilometers from the city center. The spacious, new facility helps speed your clearance through immigration and customs, but once in the arrivals lobby, a decision must be made as to how to make the long trip to Tokyo. Most convenient is the **limousine bus**, which departs just outside the lobby at frequent intervals for the Tokyo City Air Terminal (TCAT), from where you can take a taxi or walk to one of two nearby subway stations (Kayabacho or Ningyocho on the Hibiya Line) to reach your final destination. The trip takes about 70 minutes. The fare is ¥2,500, and you purchase your ticket from a well-marked booth in front of the customs-area exit.

A cheaper — and sometimes more reliable — way is the **Keisei Line Skyliner** non-stop express train, which departs from the Keisei Airport Station a short distance from the terminal by bus for Ueno Station, not far from the city center. The fare is ¥1,460, including the bus trip from terminal to station at Narita. The trains depart about every half hour, and the trip takes exactly one hour. Tickets can be purchased at a booth to the right as you exit from the customs-area exit in the arrivals lobby, or at the Keisei Airport Station.

PRICES

All prices listed in this book were accurate as of mid-1982. In this inflationary world, however, kindly plan to pay a little more than listed, and be pleased if the figures quoted are close to accurate.

TOKYO

TOKYO: THROBBING NERVE CENTER

At first glance Tokyo looks like a great, gray blob of concrete, steel, glass, stucco and flimsy wood. Then the little things begin to come into focus: a finely pruned pine tree gracefully draped over a stone wall; some petite well-dressed bar hostess on her way to work in the Ginza; a piece of crude pottery filled with only a wheat stalk in a shop window; some winding lane full of bobbing, red paper lanterns; a sumo wrestler in kimono, his hair in a topknot, making a telephone call on a street corner. Little thing by little thing, Tokyo envelops even the casual, short-time visitor with her charms.

This is Japan's "Big Apple", the ultimate destination for the over-achievers in a land where over-achieving is a mania. The nation's top businessmen, politicians, artists, writers, actors, intellectuals — all those talented people that make any great city great — converge here to give Tokyo a throbbing life matched by few other urban areas in the world. In population, area covered, wealth, abundance of artistic objects and its role in world affairs, Tokyo stands right up there with New York, London or Paris. Beyond that, comparisons fail.

Big city sophistication abounds, but the overall impression of the man in the street is that he still has one foot back in the rice paddy of his home village. The jaded ways of the west are becoming more tempting to Mr. Yamamoto, but he hasn't yet been able to shake off his wide-eyed innocence. For the hard-boiled New Yorker or Parisian, this makes Tokyo nothing short of refreshing.

Country ethics prevail. No one thinks of himself/herself so much as a Tokyoite than as a resident of some little neighborhood not really so different than his/her birthplace. Each area has its ma-and-pa grocers, tailors, barbers, public bath and shrine — the latter all but ignored, except during festival time. He/she may work in Marunouchi, the city's "Wall Street", or in the Ginza. But the heart lies way out there in Takasago or Ogikubo.

For a big city, things shut down surprisingly early. The last movie starts at 6:30 or 7 p.m. Concerts ditto. Most restaurants close by 9 p.m. The buses stop running around 10 p.m., and the trains stop shortly after midnight.

By Japanese standards Tokyo is a relatively new city, not really finding its place in history until Tokugawa Ieyasu made Yedo or Edo, Tokyo's old name, the nation's administrative center by setting up his government here at the beginning of the 17th century. The *Shogun*'s samurai retainers followed, along with the regional feudal lords who were required to maintain second homes in Edo, plus the craftsmen who came to make beautiful things for the rich and the merchants who knew an opportunity when they saw it.

By the mid-18th century the city had an estimated population of over one million, with London being its only rival. It hasn't stopped growing since. An extra burst of life came when the Emperor Meiji established himself in Edo in 1868, making it the official capital and renaming it Tokyo (east capital).

Since the city was practically flattened by the fire bombings of World War II, there is little old that remains. Save your temple and shrine viewing for Kyoto and Nara. But today, just 37 years after the holocaust, Tokyo glitters as never before. Earthquakes, fires, wars — this metropolis has seen them all, but she's never been long in recuperating.

Perhaps the most beguiling quality about Tokyo for the foreigner is that it offers both a taste of East and West. There's *kabuki*, but there are also films from America and Europe. You can attend a concert by a famous western artist, or go to a *koto* (Japanese harp) recital. Japanese food is everywhere, but just around the corner there is a chic little restaurant where — for a price — you can have a French meal almost as tasty as in Paris. Tokyo has an eclecticism that's hard to beat.

GETTING YOUR BEARINGS

The problem is sorting out what suits you from the rich abundance, then finding it. Start by stopping at JNTO's

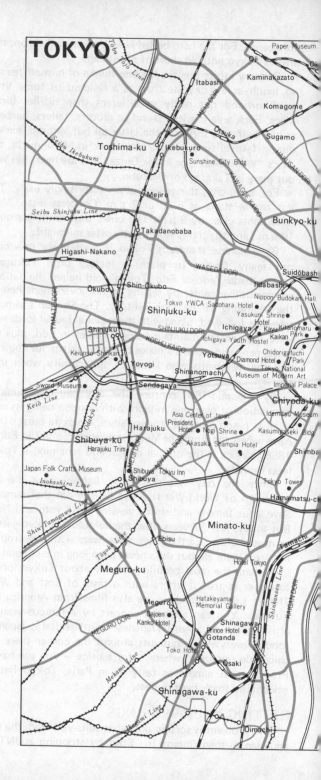

TOKYO

Paper Museum
Oji
Ok
Itabashi
Kaminakazato
Toei Tojo Line
Komagome
Otsuka
Sugamo
Seibu Ikebukuro
Toshima-ku
Ikebukuro
Sunshine City Bldg
HAKUSAN DORI
KAWAGOE KAIDO
Mejiro
Seibu Shinjuku Line
Bunkyo-ku
Takadanobaba
Higashi-Nakano
WASEDA DORI
Suidobashi
Edogawabashi
Iidabashi
Okubo
Shin-Okubo
Nippon Budokan Hall
Tokyo YWCA Sadohara Hotel
Shinjuku-ku
Yasukuni Shrine
Hotel
Ichigaya
Kayu Kitanomaru
Kaikan Park
Shinjuku
SHINJUKU DORI
KOSHU KAIDO
Ichigaya Youth Hostel
Keiunso-Shinkan
Chidorigafuchi
Yoyogi
Yotsuya
Diamond Hotel
Park
Tokyo National
Shinanomachi
Museum of Modern Art
Sword Museum
Sendagaya
Imperial Palace
Keio Line
Odakyu Line
Chiyoda-ku
Idemitsu Museum
Asia Center of Japan
President
Harajuku
Hotel
Nogi Shrine
Kasumigaseki Bldg
Shibuya-ku
Akasaka Shampia Hotel
Harajuku Trim
MEIJI DORI
Shimba
Japan Folk Crafts Museum
Inokashira Line
Shibuya Tokyu Inn
Shibuya
Tokyo Tower
Shin-Tamagawa Line
Hamamatsu-c
Toyoko Line
Minato-ku
Ebisu
Tamachi
Hotel Tokyo
Shinkansen Line
Meguro-ku
KAIGAN DORI
Meguro
Hatakeyama
Memorial Gallery
Gajoen
Kanko Hotel
Shinagawa
MEGURO DORI
Prince Hotel
Gotanda
Toko Hotel
Mekama Line
Osaki
Shinagawa-ku
Ikegami Line
Oimachi

28

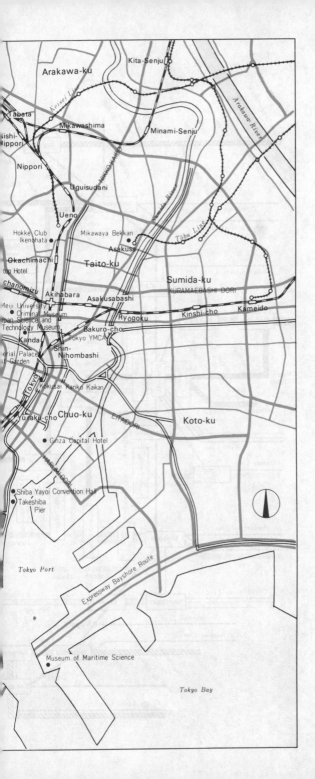

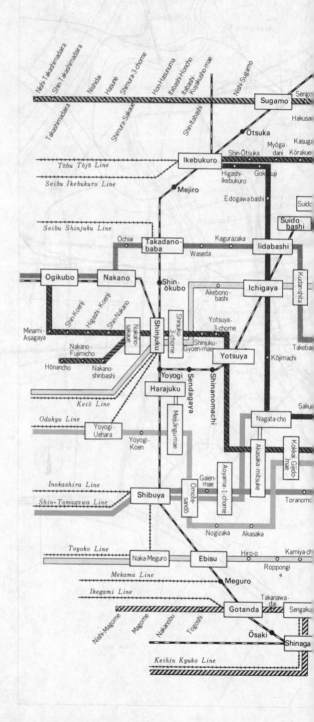

Tokyo Rail-Subway Network

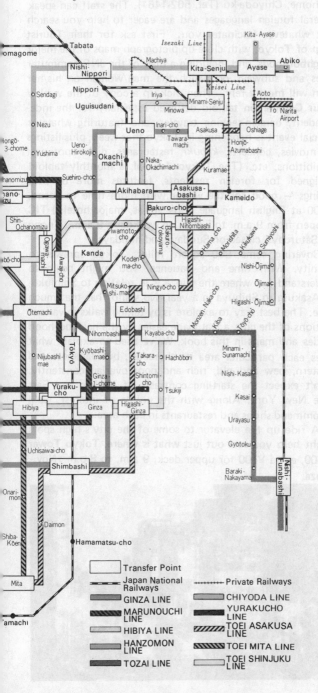

	Transfer Point
	Japan National Railways
....	Private Railways
	GINZA LINE
	CHIYODA LINE
	MARUNOUCHI LINE
	YURAKUCHO LINE
	HIBIYA LINE
	TOEI ASAKUSA LINE
	HANZOMON LINE
	TOEI MITA LINE
	TOZAI LINE
	TOEI SHINJUKU LINE

Tourist Information Center (TIC) located near Yurakucho Station, Hibiya, in the Kotani Bldg., 6-6, Yurakucho 1-chome, Chiyoda-ku (Tel. 502-1461). The staff can speak several foreign languages and are eager to help you search out whatever fascinates you. First ask for their **Tourist Map of Tokyo**, with close-up pictograph maps of the major neighborhoods, and including a map of the JNR commuter lines and subways on which the man/woman on his/her own will mostly rely. Then pick up a copy of the weekly **Tour Companion** tabloid designed especially for the independent, bargain-seeking traveler, and featuring whatever special event is happening in Tokyo that week, plus listings of movies, concerts, *kabuki*, restaurants, night spots, art exhibitions, etc. (The **Tokyo Journal**, a monthly tabloid designed for foreign residents, features more off-beat listings — good for the visitor with more time to spend. ¥200 at English language book stores, major hotels.) TIC is open from 9 a.m. to 5 p.m. on weekdays, 9 a.m. to noon on Saturdays, closed on Sundays and holidays.

Covering some 800 square miles, Tokyo sprawls to infinity. With time and patience, you might begin to understand just where the Ginza is in relation to Shinjuku, or Asakusa to Shibuya in a year. No visitor has that much time. The best way to explore is by taking walks in various sections of the city, a feat made easier by the neighborhood guides and maps in this book. We've tried to explain what gives each particular area its character, but Japanese and western, new and old, rich and poor overlap constantly. Don't expect the startling contrasts of Harlem and East Side New York. Along with the points of interest, we'll recommend shops and restaurants in each area.

A ride up the elevator to some of the city's high spots might help you sort out just what is where. **Tokyo Tower** (¥600, extra ¥400 for upper deck, 9 a.m. to 8 p.m.; Nov.-

Ginza

Mar., 6 p.m.) offers the best view of the bay and harbor. The observation floor of the **Kasumigaseki Bldg.** (free) in the government office district offers the supreme view down into the Imperial Palace compound, about as close as you can get to these highly secluded grounds. **Sunshine City Bldg.** ¥600, 10 a.m.-7:30 p.m.), now the city's tallest at 60 stories in Ikebukuro, offers a good view of the Tanzawa Mountains and Mt. Fuji beyond to the west.

For what it's worth, like most of the many Japanese castle towns Tokyo grew out in concentric circles from the castle which was first the *shogun*'s residence, later the Emperor's. The moat closest to the castle walls remains, and you can make a complete circle around the great stone walls in about an hour. This is a favorite course for the city's joggers. The next in the former circle of moats is still visible at Akasaka-Mitsuke below the New Otani Hotel and from Yotsuya past Ichigaya to Iidabashi, a path lined with cherry blossoms in April.

The favored picture-taking spot at the Imperial Palace is **Nijubashi Bridge** with a turret from the former Fushimi Castle at Kyoto perched on the wall above it. With your back to the bridge, follow busy Uchibori Dori to your left until you come to Otemon Gate, through which you can enter the **East Garden**, site of the main buildings of the old castle, between 9 a.m. and 4 p.m. everyday except Mondays and Fridays. You can exit from the East Garden through the Kita Hanebashimon Gate, across the street from which you'll find **Kitanomaru Park**, home of three fine museums, plus **Nippon Budokan Hall**, a modern arena for Japanese martial arts as well as rock concerts. The **Tokyo National Museum of Modern Art** (¥250, 10 a.m. to 5 p.m.; Fri., 8 p.m., closed Mon.) has a permanent collection of Japanese art of the last 100 years and usually a special exhibition of some 20th century western artist lodged on its main floor. This museum also has a separate **Crafts Galley** (¥250, 10 a.m. to 5 p.m., closed Mon.) devoted to Japanese modern crafts and housed in what was formerly the 19th century home of the Imperial Palace guards up the hill and inside the park from the main museum. This is a good starting place for studying Japan's rich tradition in folk art. Also inside the park is the **Science and Technology Museum** (¥500, 9:30 a.m. to 4:50 p.m.), no threat to the great science museums in Chicago or Munich, but adequate for science enthusiasts.

Across the moat to the west of Kitanomaru Park is **Chidorigafuchi Park**, famous for the cherry blossoms in season. And just north of Chidorigafuchi is **Yasukuni Shrine**, devoted to Japan's war dead, noted for its 66-foot-high bronze gate at the main entrance. This shrine is one of the main gathering places for Japanese during the New Year's holidays.

East of the Imperial Palace compound lie the **Ginza-Marunouchi** districts, the closest thing to a city-center this city with many centers has. Almost all of the subway (called *chika tetsu*) system's 10 lines pass through or near these areas like spokes on a bicycle wheel. The subway, along with the JNR Yamanote and Sobu Lines which connect with the subway at various points, will be your prime means of getting around, and a word on how to use the system will be helpful.

Tickets for both the subway and JNR lines are purchased from a vending machine outside the station's entrance(s). The fares are based on distance traveled, so you'll have to refer to the map above the machines to find out the fare to your particular destination.

At stations frequented by foreigners, there is usually a small map with the stations written in Roman letters posted somewhere. If not, you can match your map in Roman letters with the one in Chinese and Japanese characters above.

Don't worry. In any case, if you didn't pay enough, the ticket man who will take your ticket at your destination will tell you what the difference is. If you paid too much, however, the loss is yours. Currently fares on the subway are somewhat cheaper than the JNR lines.

JNR's Yamanote Line makes a wide loop through the Ginza-Marunouchi districts at Shimbashi, Yurakucho and Tokyo stations, and on around through the major transfer terminals of Ueno, Ikebukuro, Shinjuku, Shibuya and Shinagawa where commuters switch to other lines for the distant suburbs. The Sobu line is convenient for reaching points in central Tokyo between Akihabara and Shinjuku.

Tokyo's buses generally run between the subway lines and sometimes will take you much closer to your destination than the trains. The buses all have numbers, but signs on the buses and at most bus stops are not posted in Roman letters. If you must use a bus, get your directions clearly from a Japanese before you leave, or pick up a copy of "The Great Tokyo Detailed Map" published by Nippon Kokuseisha Co., Ltd. at an English-language book store. The map shows Tokyo bus routes marked by their corresponding numbers. The fare is ¥140, regardless of distance. A machine at the entrance will give you change for ¥150 or ¥200. No bills.

Finally, there are taxis everywhere, and the drivers are eager to stop at the wave of your hand. Fares start at ¥430 for the first 2 km., however, and a trip between the Ginza and Roppongi areas, for example, can easily push the meter up to ¥1,000. Handy they are, but a few taxi rides can easily wreck a small travel budget. The drivers rarely speak English and, unlike most cities, seldom know any but the most common destinations. The passenger must often guide them block by block, no easy task if you can't speak Japanese. Always allow for more time than you think you need, and don't tip.

GINZA-NIHOMBASHI

Contrary to foreign understanding, Ginza is not a street, but a whole district distinguished by day, along with the nearby Nihombashi district, as the capital's and the nation's chief center of high fashion and luxury goods, including the greatest concentration of art galleries; and by night for perhaps the most expensive night life in the world.

For the city's old-rich, never as distinguishable as their counterparts in the West, and new-rich, as flashy as anywhere, the Ginza is simply IT. Class consciousness is discreet in Japan. The majority think of themselves as middle class, and by American and European standards, they are. But tycoons and old aristocrats, if not obvious, are still on the scene, and the Ginza is where you're most apt to find them.

The best introduction is a leisurely stroll at dusk when the sky is a lavender glow and those famed neon signs begin flashing their commercial messages — veritable dreams for color fans and typographers. This is Tokyo's best hour when the millions of office workers begin pouring out of their companies, through the streets and into the thousands of bars, many no bigger than walk-in closets.

Tokyo night life and bar life come in many forms. The Ginza variety includes some big-name night clubs with floor shows similar to those of any city in the world; some *nomiya*, the Japanese style drinking places where the junior staff gather for booze and tidbits; and a great number of hostess bars, the modern-day version of the geisha houses of old.

There are hostess bars all over Tokyo, of course, but none quite so classy as those in the Ginza, and none so much aspired to by the ladies of the profession. Quite simply, this is where the big money is spent, most of it from the lavish expense accounts of major companies. With few exceptions, the girls are in the business for money first and foremost, along with the common dream among Japanese women of finding someone to take care of them. For the bar hostess, this means playing mistress to some company top executive and maybe one day having her own bar.

35

The Ginza bars close between 11:30 p.m. and 12 midnight, and the late-night rush-hour is a sight unmatched anywhere. Those black limousines with the white seat covers and the thousands of taxis, each waiting for some bleary-eyed executive to come lumbering out into the street, make the streets impassable. The mama-sans follow their customers right out and bow them away with a gush of thank-yous.

The following two suggested walking tours wind from Hibiya Park to Tsukiji, and from the main Ginza intersection to the Mitsukoshi Department Store's headquarters in Nihombashi. Both can be done in half a day, if you're a fast mover. But a full day offers a more leisurely pace. Ginza shops are open from 11 a.m. to 8 p.m., department stores to 6 p.m.

Hibiya Park was the city's first western-style public park and, like so many parks and gardens in Tokyo, was formerly a feudal lord's mansion. It's a popular picnic lunch spot for office workers on weekdays and, since it's one of the few parks without a wall around it and a late-afternoon closing time, one of the more active parks after dark.

Across the street is the **Imperial Hotel**, Tokyo's grand-daddy of the western hotels and especially famous to foreigners when the site was occupied by a Mayan monolith designed by American architect Frank Lloyd Wright. Today its new building would be equally at home in any western city. The basement shopping arcade is smart — and expensive — but great for window shoppers.

Exit at the side entrance and turn right. Across the street is the **Takarazuka Theater**, Tokyo home for the all-girl revue popularized by James Michener in his novel "Sayonara". For reasons understood only by students of Japanese psychology, these revues are frequented not by men, but by teen-age girls in bobby sox, who have been known to wait in line all night to get the best seats for their favorite stars. Ticket prices range from ¥700 to ¥3,000 and the show is recommended for spectacular costumes and staging. Curtain times are 1 and 5:30 p.m. on weekdays, no matinee on Mon. or Fri.; 11 a.m. and 3:30 p.m. on Sun. and hol. Takarazuka performances are held during the months of March, April, July, August, November and December only. Other stage productions are held at the theater during the remaining months.

Further down the street flanking the Imperial Hotel is **T. Sakai**, a favorite for woodblock prints. Quality originals are scarce, but the shop is one of the best in town for reproductions of the most popular prints. Under the railroad tracks on both sides of the street is the **International Arcade**, also fun for tourists. **Hayashi Kimono** on the right is recommended for old kimono and *obi*, used by foreign ladies for dressing gowns and table center runners respectively.

On the other side of the tracks and on the right is the New Riccar Building where you'll find the **Riccar Art Museum** (¥300, 11 a.m. to 6 p.m., closed Mon.) specializing in *ukiyo-e* old Japanese woodblock prints. At the next corner is the **Gallery Center Bldg.** with seven floors of art galleries. It's a convenient stop to survey the Tokyo art scene.

Turn left at the next big intersection onto Sotobori Dori, marked with a sign in Roman letters. This street is commonly known as Dentsu Dori, because it holds some of the offices of Japan's gigantic advertising agency Dentsu. One block to the left at the intersection with Harumi Dori is one of the city's more awesome displays of neon. The **Sony Bldg.** is a landmark and favorite rendezvous point. It serves as a showroom for Sony products, and the upper floors, as well as the basements, hold boutiques and restaurants — the most famous of which is the Tokyo branch of Paris' Maxim's.

Retrace your steps along Sotobori Dori toward Shimbashi Station. The avenue is lined with art galleries. Three blocks ahead on the left is **Takumi Craft Shop**, a good introduction to Japan's flourishing folk art industry, including rustic pottery, paper-covered boxes, papier mâché toys, fabrics and furniture. Just ahead is the Nikko Hotel from where you take a left into the narrow street. Straight ahead on Namiki Dori is **S. Watanabe**, one of several galleries in Tokyo specializing in modern woodblock prints and graphic arts, great favorites of the city's foreign community and

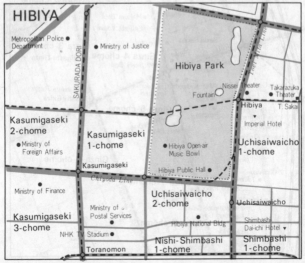

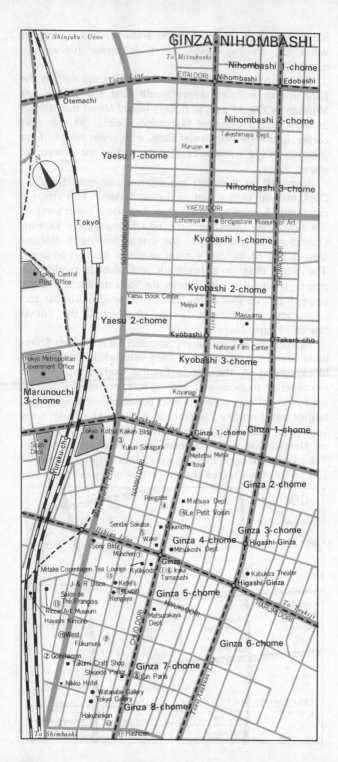

GINZA · NIHOMBASHI

To Shinjuku · Ueno

To Mitsukoshi

Tozai Line — EITAIDORI — Nihombashi — Edobashi

Nihombashi 1-chome

Otemachi

Nihombashi 2-chome
■ Takashimaya Dept.

Yaesu 1-chome
Maruzen ■

Nihombashi 3-chome

YAESUDORI

Tōkyō

Echizenya ■ ● Bridgestone Museum of Art

Kyobashi 1-chome

● Tokyo Central
Post Office

Kyobashi 2-chome
Yaesu Book Center ●
Meijiya ■

Mayuyama ■

Yaesu 2-chome
Kyōbashi ○

Takara-cho ●

National Film Center ●

Tokyo Metropolitan
Government Office

Kyobashi 3-chome

Marunouchi
3-chome

Koyanagi ●

Yūrakuchō Line

Tokyo Kotsu Kaikan Bldg
③ Yukun Sakagura

Ginza 1-chome ○ Ginza 1-chome

Sogo
Dept

Meitetsu Melsa ●
Itoya ●

Ginza 2-chome

Namikidori

Rengatei ■ Matsuya Dept
④   ⑯ Le Petit Voisin

Hibiya Line

Sendai Sakaba
⑤   ● Mikimoto
● Wako   Ginza 4-chome   ○ Higashi-Ginza

Sony Bldg
München ⑦
Mitake Copenhagen Tea Lounge   ● Mitsukoshi Dept.
⑬   Kyūkyodo   Ginza

Ginza 3-chome

①⑥ Iraka
Tamazushi

J & R Disco   ● Ketel's
⑭ Lupin
Salon de   ◆ Rengaya
Thé François
Riccar Art Museum
Hayashi Kimono

Ginza 5-chome   Kabukiza Theater ●

Higashi-Ginza ○

MIYUKIDORI

To Tsukiji

HARUMIDORI

⑩ West   Matsuzakaya
Fukumura ⑨   Dept.

Ginza 6-chome

② Gomhacoin
■ Takumi Craft Shop
Shiseido Parlor

Ginza 7-chome

▼ Nikko Hotel

⑧ Gin Paris

● Watanabe Gallery
● Tokyo Gallery

Ginza 8-chome

Hakuhinkan
⑫

To Shimbashi

⑪ Hashizen

SOTOBORIDORI

SHOWADORI

Ginza Line

Marunouchi Line

CHUODORI

Toei Asakusa Line

tourists.

Adjacent to S. Watanabe on the second floor above the Victoria Coffee Shop is the **Tokyo Gallery**, which specializes in avant-garde, modern art. **Namiki Dori** is one of the Ginza's most fashionable avenues. As you stroll along this narrow, tree-lined street back toward the Sony Bldg., you'll pass more art galleries, dozens of smart fashion boutiques, including the Tokyo branch of Gucci, plus several well-known foreign restaurants, including **Rengaya** for French cuisine and **Ketel's** for German dishes. On the right close to busy Harumi Dori is the **Yoseido Gallery**, a pioneer establishment in the world of Japanese modern woodblock prints.

Turn right on Harumi Dori. One block before the main Ginza intersection turn right again into Suzuran Dori, another shopping lane. Half-way down the block on the right you'll spot a Scandinavian-modern tea room through the windows into the basement. This is the **Mitake Copenhagen Tea Lounge**, brought to Tokyo by those friendly Danes who have given the world their distinctive blue and white china. For ¥800 you can drop into a comfortable chair and be served a pot of their fine tea in, yes, a blue and white Royal Copenhagen pot. First class tea (also coffee) in a first-class atmosphere.

Continue on Suzuran Dori to the next corner and turn left for one block to the Ginza main street officially known as Chuo Dori. Across the street is one of the avenue's leading department stores, **Matsuzakaya** (closed Wed.).

Take a left on Chuo Dori back toward Harumi Dori, and just before you reach the distinctive glass, silo-like Sanai Bldg. at the intersection on the left you'll spot **Kyūkyodō**, famous for stationery and writing materials, which in Japan means fine brushes, not pens.

Back on Harumi Dori again, turn right and walk for about five minutes across the next main intersection. On the left is the ornate **Kabukiza Theater**, rebuilt to almost its former splendor after burning in World War II. If you're even slightly serious about live theater, don't miss seeing at least one act. Ask for a *makumi* (curtain-viewing) ticket, and for from ¥400 to ¥900 you can catch the act of your choice.

If you're a serious theater buff, make this a half-day event, because the full performance takes that long. Matinees begin at 11 a.m. and run until 4 p.m., with breaks for lunch. Evening performances start at 4:30 and last until 9:30, with a break for supper. Prices start at ¥1,500 up to ¥9,000 for the close-up seats, with 10 per cent discounts to foreigners who show their passports on the day of performance.

Performances usually consist of three parts — one classical *kabuki* story, full of swash and bravado; a 19th century "modern" work packed with melodrama (slow going for the foreigner); and a dance, easily the most understood part. All roles are played by men. English programs explaining the complicated plots of the stories are on sale for ¥600. Earphones with English commentary may be rented for ¥500.

Continuing east on Harumi Dori another 10 or 15 minutes will bring you to **Tsukiji**, the city's burgeoning fish market, which is at its busiest around 5 a.m., and a number of excellent fish restaurants where freshness is almost guaranteed. Some 70,000 dealers handle 2,500 tons of seafood per day here. If you're in the neighborhood at lunch or supper time, stop by the main shop of **Edogin** (11 a.m. to 9:30, closed Sun.), a traditional sushi shop low on looks and price but high on taste. If it's still wiggling, you

Kabukiza Theater

know it's fresh. Ten pieces of raw fish over vinegared rice balls (*nigiri zushi*) plus beer or sake will cost between ¥3,000 to ¥4,000.

The second walk in the Ginza-Nihombashi districts takes you from Mitsukoshi to Mitsukoshi, the Ginza main intersection branch of what's perhaps Japan's most famous department store, to the main store at Nihombashi.

Skip the Ginza branch of Mitsukoshi and save your energy for the big mother store at the end of this tour. **Wako** (closed Sun.) across the street, specializes in imported fashions, jewelry and accessories — most with prices that will make your eyeballs roll. A neighbor just up the street is the **Mikimoto** store, the showcase for Japan's famous cultured pearls of the same name.

On the next block **Matsuya** (closed Thurs.) is a pacesetter in introducing European and American designs. Its "Craft Gallery" on the sixth floor offers modern Japanese crafts by young designers, while the "Design Collection" on seventh has the latest European designs in household goods.

In the middle of the next block on the right are seven floors of novelties at **Ito-ya**, which specializes in stationery, household gadgets, *origami* paper, drawing and graphics supplies, and more.

A good place to examine Japanese everyday, ceramic house wares is **Koyanagi**, which has been in operation for over 100 years in the next block on the left. You can pick up some original and inexpensive gift such as a tiny pair of chopstick rests for a few hundred yen here.

Continue on Chuo Dori beneath the expressway to the Kyobashi intersection, marked by another subway station entrance, with the name written in Roman letters. Turn right and a few minutes up the block on the right is the **National Film Center** which shows old film revivals at 3:00 and 6:15 p.m. everyday except Sundays, the program changing everyday. This is the one revival theater in Tokyo where the Japanese films on view may have English subtitles. But not always. The programs are not printed in English. Ask a Japanese to call 561-0823 to find out what's playing. The price is just ¥250.

Now cross the wide boulevard in front of the Center and enter the narrow street with more art galleries just to the right. **Mayuyama** on your left has a history of over 70-years and is Tokyo's oldest antique shop. It's especially rich in Japanese, Chinese and Korean ceramics and the staff are friendly and happy to show you around, if you show serious interest.

41

TOKYO STATION

Continue on this narrow street past other galleries and small shops to Yaesu Dori, the next wide boulevard, and turn left. At the end of this avenue you'll spot the modern side of busy **Tokyo Station**, where an average of 2,500 trains depart each day (compared with about 500 at New York's Grand Central). Just before you reach the next big intersection in the headquarters of the Bridgestone Tire Co., Japan's answer to Firestone, is the **Bridgestone Museum of Art** (¥300, 10 a.m. to 5:30 p.m., closed Mon.), famous in Tokyo for its French impressionist collection, but more interesting to foreigners for works by Japanese artists who were influenced by the impressionists.

Take a right at the big intersection, and you're back on Chuo Dori, just a few short blocks from **Takashimaya** (closed Wed.) which the Japanese claim is the best for western goods and which foreign residents admire because its style of merchandising is like the department stores back home. Especially interesting are the cavernous food halls in the basement, and in the rear on the same floor are a series of small shops featuring Oriental curios and antiques. A floor-by-floor guide in English is available from the girls at the information counters who are smartly dressed, as are the elevator operators, to suit the season.

Across the street is **Maruzen** (closed Sun.), another department store, but noted chiefly for its foreign language book section on third floor, the largest and most convenient in this part of the city. On the same floor don't miss **Craft Center Japan,** a corner devoted to good Japanese modern design.

Continue on Chuo Dori to **Nihombashi Bridge**, which was the hub from which all distances in Japan were measured during the Edo era. The current bridge dates from 1912— more Victorian than Japanese.

Just over the bridge and one more block on the left is the **Mitsukoshi** (closed Mon.) mother store, its distinctive fuchsia and white wrapping paper a sign to the gift receiver that the giver has sought the very best. The main floor is dominated by a giant sculpture of the goddess of sincerity, assuring customers they'll get a fair deal. The store features boutiques of many shops from back home, including Cartier and Tiffany's.

This completes your look at Ginza-Nihombashi, Tokyo's sparkling retail heart, an enticing combination of traditional Japanese good taste and the latest fashions from the west.

GINZA EATS, DRINKS & MUSIC

❶ **Tamazushi** (築地玉寿司 銀座5-8銀座コアビル, Tel. 573-0057)
This Ginza branch of a 50-year-old Tsukiji *sushi* shop packs them in for low-cost, tasty raw fish. Squeeze in at the counter and start pointing. ¥1,500 - ¥2,000. B2 of the Ginza Core Bldg. near the main Ginza crossing. 11 a.m.-10 p.m.

❷ **Gomihacchin** (五味八珍 銀座8-2-16, Tel. 571-2486)
The specialty is *kushiage* - meat and seasonal vegetables dipped in a batter and deep-fried - and the atmosphere is Japanese rustic with a bevy of old lamps, China and glass, plus Christian emblems familiar to Kyushu feudal lords. No menu. Ask for the *teishoku*, a set course of several skewers with rice, or say *"moriawase kudasai,"* and they'll give you a variety of whatever is available. Shout *stoppu* (stop) when you've had enough, or the bill will keep climbing. Average ¥4,000. 4-10 p.m., closed Sun., hol.

❸ **Yūkun Sakagura** (有薫酒蔵 銀座2-2, Tel. 561-6672)
Kyushu country food inside a folk-style basement room resembling a sake brewery by stage-designer Kisaku Ito. Low-priced, tasty *teishoku* - Yukun *teishoku* - (a box of cold delicacies); *onigiri* (rice balls wrapped in seaweed) or *udon* (thick noodles) at ¥750, ¥550 and ¥550 respectively - from 11:30 a.m.-1 p.m. Around ¥3,000 from 5-10 p.m. No English sign outside. Entrance beside Meitetsu World Travel across from Yuraku Food Center. Closed Sun., hol.

❹ **Rengatei** (煉瓦亭 銀座3-5-16, Tel. 561-7515)
This is a Ginza old-timer serving the Japanese idea of western food, and popular with shoppers and salary men. The jumbo pork cutlet at ¥1,300 is perhaps the tastiest. 11 a.m.-3 p.m.; 4:30-9 p.m., closed Sun.

❺ **Sendai Sakaba** (仙台酒場 銀座4-4-13, Tel. 564-2081)
Northern Honshu cuisine, with fish stews as the specialties in the winter months, amid the Tohoku region's *kokeshi* dolls. The English sign says "Japanese Public Bar Sendai," and this basement room is just off Harumi Dori on the right side of the street leading from Tenshodo jewelers. 4:30-10 p.m., closed Sun., hol.

❻ **Iraka** (甍 銀座5-8銀座コアビル, Tel. 572-8465)
Kansai-style (Osaka area) goodies, easy to select from the plastic models in the window. B2 of Ginza Core Bldg. ¥1,500 - ¥3,000. 11 a.m.-10 p.m.

❼ **München Beer Hall**
(ミュンヘン・ピア・ホール 銀座5-6-2, Tel. 571-3829)
Munchen beer, German music, the waitresses in German country costumes, and a wide variety of Japanese-style German dishes looking and tasting nothing like the real thing. A basement room, the entrance just beside Ando Cloisonne on Harumi Dori. ¥1,000 and up. 3-10 p.m.

❽ **Gin Paris** (銀巴里 銀座7-9-11, Tel. 571-0085)
Japan's up and coming *chanson* singers draw steady crowds to this theater-style basement room. Pay ¥1,200, plus ¥400 for coffee or

more for booze, at the door, and you can sit here forever dreaming of Paris. Just off the Ginza main street across from the Shiseido Boutique Bldg. Weekdays, 5:30-10 p.m.; Sat. 1:30-10 p.m.; Sun. and hol. 1:30-9 p.m.

⑨ Fukumura (富久むら 銀座7-6, Tel. 571-0737)

Oden, a vegetable dumpling stew, is a great winter-time warmer-upper. Point to what you want over the counter. A favorite with painters and writers. On Ginza 5th St. across the street from the Pub Ocean 7. 4-10 p.m., closed Sun., hol.

⑩ West (ウェスト 銀座7-3-6, Tel. 571-2989)

Perhaps the classiest tea room in all the Ginza. White linen, fresh flowers and classical music. Popular with shoppers by day; bar hostesses by night. On Dentsu Dori and easy to spot, because the shop's bake goods are sold from the front window. Also Aoyama, Meguro and Harajuku. 9 a.m.-1 a.m.; Sun. from noon.

⑪ Hashizen (橋善 新橋1-7-11, Tel. 571-2700)

A tempura shop with a 150-year history. *Kakiage donburi,* a deep fried patty of white fish, shell fish and vegetables over rice, is the specialty. On the main Ginza street just south of the overhead expressway near Shimbashi Station. 11 a.m.-8:30 p.m.; Sun. 12-8 p.m.

⑫ Hakuhinkan Theater (博品館 銀座8-8-11, Tel. 571-1003)

This small theater on the 8th floor of the Hakuhinkan Bldg. on the main Ginza street beside the expressway offers shades of off-Broadway far from New York, but at Broadway prices from ¥2,000-¥5,000. Drama and musical reviews are always changing. The language is Japanese. Ask a Japanese friend to call and find out what's playing.

⑬ J & R Disco (J & R ディスコ 銀座5-4-9, Tel. 572-7383)

The Japanese sportswear company Jun operates this disco on the 6th floor of their Namiki Dori fashion boutique, and it's popular with young lovelies. 6-11 p.m.; Fri., Sat., 11:30 p.m.

⑭ Lupin (ルパン 銀座5-5-11, Tel. 571-0750)

In the alley behind Ketel's German restaurant, this bar dating from 1928 is a gathering place for the intellegentsia and attracts some of the most serious-looking faces in town. 5-11 p.m., closed Sun.

⑮ Salon de Thé François

(フランソア喫茶室 銀座6-3-11, Tel. 572-1779)

European ambience, good coffee and cake, and view of the bar hostesses going to and from work. Located on the second floor above the Roger & Gallet boutique. 9:30 a.m.-1 a.m.; Sun. from 11 a.m.

⑯ Le Petit Voisin

(プティボワザン 銀座3-6-1松屋銀座8F, Tel. 567-1375)

The portions are miniscule, but the taste is great at this cozy French bistro on the 8th floor Restaurant City of Matsuya Dept. A branch of a popular French restaurant at Kudanshita. ¥2,000 - ¥3,000 special lunches. ¥5,000 average in evening. 11:30 a.m.-9:30 p.m., closed Thurs. Special entrance on main Ginza street after 6 p.m. Matsuya closing hour.

ASAKUSA

If the spirit of old Japan survives anywhere in Tokyo, you'll find it in *shitamachi,* Tokyo's "downtown" neighborhoods, meaning down by the several wide rivers that flow into Tokyo Bay — the Sumida, Arakawa and Edogawa.

This is where the *Edokko,* or true Tokyoites of at least three generations, still live, and here are preserved two qualities the Japanese still hold dear — *giri* (a sense of obligation to others) and *ninjo* (empathy).

The spiritual heart of *shitamachi* is Asakusa, and especially around **Sensoji Temple**, more popularly known as **Asakusa Kannon** for the *Kannon,* or goddess of mercy, enshrined. This neighborhood bursts with life at anytime, but during the many festivals held here, it's especially spirited.

At the Sanja Festival on the third Sat. and Sun. in May, for example, the area residents, mostly laborers, bound through the narrow streets carrying one-ton portable shrines from their city blocks. Each group jostles the other with hearty insults, all meant in fun. Japanese macho is in great display — tatooed men looking tough and wearing nothing but their loin cloths. The geisha strut around in high wooden clogs and with their heads crowned with 25-pound wigs. This is what Japan used to be, and still is, where westernization hasn't completely obliterated it.

This neighborhood looks, well, almost old — at least

compared with the flashier uptown sections. The folks here still take pride in maintaining their wooden houses, despite the cost of maintenance these days. Sensoji was rebuilt after being damaged in the last World War, but it looks not so different than before. And the raucous entertainment district full of vaudeville shows, third-rate striptease, porno movies and Turkish baths appeals to the earthy tastes of the area residents as it always has.

This just may be the Tokyo neighborhood you remember best, because it's nothing like your own hometown.

Asakusa Station is the last stop on the Ginza subway line. A more interesting way to get there is by the Tokyo—to Kanko kisen *suijo* water taxis which ply the Sumida River about every 30 minutes between 9:50 a.m. and 4:45 p.m. daily from either Takeshiba Pier (10 minutes by foot east of Hamamatsucho Station) or the Hama Rikyu Park boat landing (10 or 15 minutes east of Shimbashi Station) to Azuma Bridge, Asakusa (you can also return from Azuma Bridge). It's a 35-minute trip from Takeshiba Pier and costs ¥480. The tea houses which once lined the river have long ago been replaced with a condrete embankment, but the mini-cruise still has its moments, especially for bridge and engineering lovers.

From Asakusa boat landing or the station follow the wide avenue west away from the river. Across the street from the Tobu Station is the **Kamiya Bar**, which claims to be Tokyo's first "western" bar. The Victorian atmosphere has vanished, but its homemade specialty known as "Electric Brandy" is still guzzled at ¥200 a shot. Just down the street is the big gate under which hangs a giant paper lantern flanked by the gods of wind and thunder who protect the *Kannon*. It's known as **Kaminarimon**, and it leads to the temple past a long alley named **Nakamise Dori** of open-front shops, some with the usual tourist junk, but some with true specialties including fans and tortoise shell hair ornaments for geisha's wigs — or you, if your hair is thick enough to hold them.

Through Hozomon Gate, decorated with giant straw sandals, lies **Asakusa Kannon**, the main hall holding a tiny gold image of the Buddhist goddess. Out front is a copper incense burner, the smoke from which is supposed to keep you healthy and free from accidents.

Follow the wide path, usually lined with outdoor stalls selling clothing, to the left as you face the temple. This will lead you to the heart of the "gay" quarter, in the old-fashioned and somehow very appropriate sense of the word. You'll soon come to a wide cross-street full of second-run feature films and porno flicks at prices cheaper than uptown.

For ¥1,600 you can see the Japanese version of a vaudeville show — mostly stand-up comedians, singers and acrobats — at the **Shochiku Engei Hall** with an entrance on the same pedestrian mall.

ASAKUSA EATS & DRINKS

❶ Kuremutsu （暮六つ 浅草2-2-13, Tel. 842-0906)
In an alley just east of Hozomon Gate, entrance to Sensoji Temple. Drinking country style around the hearth. The walls are decorated with folk art from all over Japan. Drinks (sake or beer), plus a fresh fish from the tank for about ¥3,000. 4-9:30 p.m., closed Thurs.

❷ Nakasei （中清 浅草1-39-13, Tel. 841-7401)
At the end of another alley, this one just off the next wide street west of the Nakamise Dori. A favorite with *tempura* connoisseurs, including the late writer Kafu Nagai, with the *tempura teishoku* (*tempura* lunch of the day) from ¥2,000 at tables, ¥6,000 in tatami room. As pleasant for its teahouse atmosphere as for the deep-fried seafood and vegetables. 12-8 p.m., closed Tues.

Sanja Festival

❸ Yonekyu（米久 浅草2-17-10, Tel. 841-6416）

In the covered street arcade which leads north from the theater promenade. *Sukiyaki* for from ¥1,500, served at low tables in a large *tatami* room. This old restaurant is easily distinguished by the red porch outside. Uses prized Omi beef. 12-9 p.m., closed Tues.

❹ Matsuki（松喜 雷門2-17, Tel. 841-0298）

Another *sukiyaki* specialty spot, prices beginning at ¥2,000. 10 a.m. -8:30 p.m., closed Wed.

❺ Otafuku（大多福 千束1-6-2, Tel. 871-2521）

Asakusa's oldest *oden* palace, with over 40 varieties of vegetable and fish-cake dumplings to pick from, ¥1,500 to ¥2,000. 5-11 p.m., closed Mon.

❻ Namiki（並木 雷門2-11-9, Tel. 841-1340）

The area's most famous noodle restaurant, easily found by the bamboo trees at the entrance. *Tempura soba* (buckwheat noodles with *tempura* on top) a big seller. ¥1,000 to ¥1,500. 11:30 a.m. to 8 p.m., closed Thurs.

❼ Ichimon（一文 浅草3-12-6, Tel. 875-6800）

Sake is the feature — 20 different types — served in an old Japanese farm house. ¥2,500 to ¥3,000. 5-12 p.m.

MORE ASAKUSA ENTERTAINMENT

❽ Mokuba-kan（木馬館 浅草2-7-5）

Japanese story telling guaranteed to make you cry on the first floor, small-time drama performances on second. You may not understand the Japanese, but you'll enjoy watching the neighborhood grandmas wiping their eyes and sniffling. ¥700 upstairs; ¥1,000 downstairs.

❾ Rokkuza（ロック座 浅草2-10-12）

Striptease to make you scream "Put it on, put it on". ¥2,000.

❿ Fransuza（フランス座 浅草1-43）

More of the same. ¥1,500.

ASAKUSA SHOPPING

Along Nakamise Dori, try **Matsuzakaya** for hair ornaments priced from ¥350; **Kaneso** (just off Nakamise Dori) for Japanese cutlery from ¥1,000; and **Sukeroku** (near Hozomon Gate) for miniature dolls, scenes of old Edo, from ¥200 up.

Yonoya, to the left on the last wide street off Nakamise Dori before reaching Hozomon, specializes in hand-made combs of box-wood and camelia wood, all works of art and great for giving hair a luster.

It's fun to explore the **covered arcades** between the temple and Kokusai Dori. Asakusa is no western fashion center, as you'll quickly discern. Last year's styles fill the shops.

SHINJUKU

The main gateway to Tokyo's ever-growing western suburbs, Shinjuku ever grows along with the sprawl — a hodgepodge of urban life that was not many years ago made the subject of a New York Museum of Modern Art exhibit. It's a nightmare for those who like their urban landscapes well ordered, but proof of the "no planning is best" concept that chaos can be exciting.

If you can find your way out of **Shinjuku Station,** Japan's busiest through which pass more than 1.3 million passengers per day, you are half way to capturing the frenzied atmosphere. For reasons unknown, there is not a single sign in Roman letters in the exit halls of the JNR section. Take the west exit, and you're funneled into a below-ground plaza which leads to the Odakyu and Keio private railway lines, each with its own department store. Surface, and you're in Japan's only skyscraper complex — no match for Manhattan, but on its way. The west side is basically a wasteland for the tourist, except for the Keio Plaza Hotel, its lobby right out of "A Clockwork Orange".

Of more interest to the visitor is the shopping and entertainment area on the east side of the tracks. Perhaps more than any other section in Tokyo, Shinjuku exudes a feeling of youth. It's the favorite haunt for Tokyo's over 1 million students, many of whom pour in here after

dark to sample the myriad of cheap restaurants, bars and coffee shops.

The blaze of bright lights just outside the east entrance of the station rivals the Ginza for blinding splendor. The animated advertising on the **Studio Alta Bldg.** is a special treat and a traffic stopper. Follow this wide street to the right, away from the tracks, and you'll spot another giant, neon billboard over the **Sakuraya Camera Shop** which, along with the **Yodobashi Camera Shop** next door, offers the cheapest prices for camera equipment in the city. A tourist can trade in his old model here for a new one, and perhaps come out even better off than at the tax-free shops.

Shinjuku Dori passing Sakuraya is the area's main shopping drag. Beside Sakuraya sits the **Takano Fruit Parlor**, once a simple fruit stand, now a building full of a lot more than fruit. The **World Restaurant** on the sixth floor offers reasonably-priced Scandinavian, German, Indian, Mexican and Italian food, each in its own little corner. Down the street on your left is **Kinokuniya**, also full of boutiques, but most famous for books, with a large selection of foreign language books and periodicals on the fifth floor. Along with Takano, this is a favorite get-together point for Shinjuku frequenters. Kinokuniya also shows second-run art films, one of several places in the area specializing in movie revivals.

Further down the street on the left is **Isetan Department Store** (closed Wed.), very smart, very popular with the young for the latest faddy fashion from Europe and America. This is the closest thing to New York's Bloomingdales in Tokyo.

The side street next to Isetan holds a number of first-run theaters. Follow it to the left when exiting from Isetan's side entrance to the next big street Yasukuni Dori.

Across the street and to the left is **Kabuki-cho**, which stretches from here to the railroad tracks. Packed full of

Shinjuku East Exit

cinemas, restaurants, coffee shops, bars and discos, it's one of the liveliest night quarters in Tokyo. No special route is recommended. Just wander and let your good judgment be your guide. If you think you're lost, tag along behind any swarm of humanity. Inevitably, they'll eventually lead you back to Shinjuku Station.

SHINJUKU EATS, DRINKS & MUSIC

 1 Shirakawago (白川郷 歌舞伎町2-29-10, Tel. 200-5255)
A farm house with a high-pitched roof transplanted from the Japan Alps serving specialties from the Hida region of Japan. A complete dinner course from ¥4,000. Reached by the road leading from Club Fuyajyo. 1-11 p.m.

2 Kakiden (柿伝 新宿3-37安与ビル, Tel. 352-5121)
Kyoto's *kaiseki*-style food - tiny delicacies beautifully served and guaranteed to leave room for a Big Mac — is the specialty of this Japanese restaurant on the 8th and 9th floors of the building just behind "My City" on the east side of Shinjuku Station. 11 a.m. - 9 p.m.

3 Bajohai (馬上盃 新宿3-26, Tel. 356-2989)
Genghis Khan barbecue - lamb and vegetables cooked over the open fire - and *shabu shabu* (boiled meat and vegetables) in private alcoves. The beef Genghis Khan is ¥2,200; *shabu shabu*, ¥1,500. In the alley behind Mitsumine. 3-10 p.m.

4 Suzume-no-ojisan (雀の叔父さん 新宿3-17, Tel. 352-4931)
Yakitori (chicken pieces on a skewer) and stews in the ¥2,000-¥3,000 area. Just behind Kinokuniya. 3-11 p.m., closed first and third Wed. of each month.

5 Taruhei (樽平 新宿3-23-5, Tel. 354-7381)
A *tatami* room where the locals from Yamagata Prefecture gather for a taste of their region's own sake. ¥1,500-¥2,500. Unpretentiously situated on the 3rd floor, Shin Higashi Bldg., facing the east side of the railroad tracks a block off Yasukuni Dori. 4-11:30 p.m.

6 Wine Pub Tokachi
(ワインパブ十勝 新宿3-14伊勢丹デパート, Tel. 356-5946)

Shinjuku at Night

A cozy nook on the first floor of Isetan Dept., with its own entrance on Meiji Dori, serving grape wine from Hokkaido's Tokachi district, plus Hokkaido snacks like smoked salmon and baked potatoes. ¥1,000-¥2,000. 12-9 p.m., closed Wed.

❼ Akiyama （アキヤマ 西新宿1-4-9新宿西ビル， Tel. 346-2429）
Owned by the son of a famous female columnist named Chieko Akiyama, this small basement restaurant features home-made stews - oxtail (¥1,700), tongue (¥1,450), beef (¥1,350), shrimp (¥1,050), Hungarian (¥950). Special stew lunch for ¥450 between 12-3 p.m. Dinner from 4:30-10:30. In the second alley behind Odakyu Halc Dept.

❽ Volga （ボルガ 西新宿1-4， Tel. 342-4996）
You can't miss this intimate beer hall in the second alley behind Odakyu Halc Dept. Just follow your nose to the *banyaki* shish kebab being cooked over an open grill at the entrance. Beer and skewered goodies - and a bare room full of underground film directors and revolutionaries. ¥1,000-¥2,000. 5-11 p.m.

❾ Healthmagic （ヘルスマジック 新宿3-16-4， Tel. 350-5736）
Soups, pita bread sandwiches, omelettes, salads and some "gourmet entrees" geared for the health conscious. Try their high protein shake, guaranteed to bolster your energy level. ¥1,000-¥2,000 average. 11 a.m.-11 p.m.

❿ Mokuba （木馬 歌舞伎町14林ビルB2， Tel. 200-6484）
Ear-blasting recorded modern jazz amid old clocks and gramophones in the second basement of a building facing the side of Koma Theater. Coffee and cocktails in the ¥1,000 area. 12-12 p.m.

West Shinjuku

⓫ Kaizoku（海賊 新宿3-7-2, Tel. 354-3240）
Coffee or whisky (¥400), beer (¥500), gin tonic (¥600), plus a large snack menu, in a room done up like a pirate's ship. Follow the alley beside the Scalaza Theater away from Isetan. Easily spotted by the anchor at the door. 5 p.m.-1 a.m. (3 a.m. on Sat.)

⓬ Pit Inn（ピットイン 新宿3-17, Tel. 354-2024）
A live-jazz enthusiasts hangout. Performances usually between 12-2 p.m.; 3-6 p.m.; and 7-11 p.m. In the alley leading west from the west side of Isetan. ¥800-¥1,000 afternoon cover charge, including one drink; evenings, ¥1,800; special events, ¥2,000.

⓭ Cinema（シネマ 新宿3-7-6, Tel. 354-7218）
Coffee for ¥400, whiskey, beer and gin for lovers of movie soundtrack recordings and old film posters. Behind Scalaza Theater, two blocks north of Shinjuku Dori. 12-12 p.m.

⓮ Petchka（ペチカ 新宿3-15-17 伊勢丹会館, Tel. 352-3554）
Russian food is the specialty, although a Russian is not apt to recognize it. The *borscht* soup, *piroshiki* and Russian tea set lunch is a bargain at ¥600. Also Stroganoff, chicken Kiev and *shashlik*. On the 2nd floor of the Isetan Kaikan, behind and to the left of Isetan's main store. 10 a.m.-10 p.m., closed Wed.

⓯ Tsuna-Hachi（つな八 新宿3-31-8, Tel. 352-1012）
The best tempura in Shinjuku in a local landmark building with a counter, tables or *tatami* mats. Ask for their *teishoku* at around ¥1,000 - several pieces of deep fried fish and vegetables, rice, soup and pickles. On the street leading from the east end of Mitsukoshi Dept. 11:30 a.m.-9 p.m.

UENO-NIPPORI

A park full of high-brow cultural attractions, plus an adjacent neighborhood reminiscent of the Edo of old are the salient attractions of this walking tour.

Ueno Park is a meeting ground for both the cultural cognoscenti who flock to concerts at the **Tokyo Metropolitan Festival Hall** and art exhibits at three major museums, and a far greater number of citizens seeking the earthier pleasures of the zoo with its panda pair and the honky-tonk spots at the south end of the park.

Although one of the city's largest public green spots, it's the zoo and museums which are the draw, and not the lawns, which are practically nonexistent. It has neither Central Park's views of the skyscrapers through the trees nor the primness of Hyde Park.

Emerging from the north exit of Ueno Station, you'll walk right into the Festival Hall. Across from the Hall is the **National Museum of Western Art** (¥250, 9:30 a.m. to 5 p.m., closed Mon.), more interesting to the foreigner for its building designed by Le Corbusier than for the European paintings inside. Unless you've had few chances to see European art back home, save your feet for the Japanese and Far Eastern collection at the **Tokyo National Museum** (¥250, 9 a.m. to 4:30 p.m., closed Mon.) nearby.

This museum, in a compound with two other buildings, houses the greatest collection of Japanese art in the world. It includes Buddhist sculpture, textiles, woodblock prints, lacquer and metal wares, pottery and paintings on scrolls and screens. The riches are in such great number not all can be shown at one time. Another building houses Japanese prehistoric artifacts, and the third building a small collection of art from other Asian countries.

Outside the museum gate take the road to the right and follow it past the Tokyo University of Arts to the second stop light. Across the street at the right of the intersection a tiny tea-house-like shop named **Torindo** sells sugar-coated vegetables done up in lovely shapes for gifts, perhaps a nice treat for a Japanese friend, or you can tarry here for green powdered tea and cake in a set for ¥450.

Outside Torindo take a right and follow the road to the next corner. Then turn right, taking a deep breath as you pass one of the many traditional restaurants in this area —

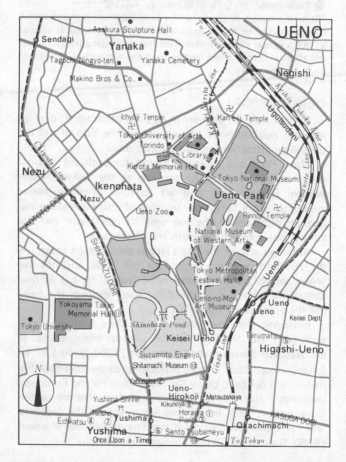

this one serving grilled eel — before the next traffic light.

Across the street on the left is Ichyōji, the first of many Buddhist temples you'll pass on the paths ahead which follow the top of a ridge. *Teramachi*, or temple towns, are common in many Japanese cities, though the reason the temples group together in a particular part of town is not very clear.

Some old Edo hands say many of the temples in this neighborhood moved out here into what was once the outskirts to avoid the frequent fires in the city proper. Since the houses and temples were made of wood, paper and straw, and heating and cooking were done with open fires, conflagrations were an everyday occurrence. Sometimes they destroyed large areas of the city.

Whatever the reason, the temples and what goes with them — wooden memorial tablets to dead ancestors, grave stones, flowers and the heady smell of incense — give a certain solemnity and dignity that is rare in modern Tokyo.

This temple road takes a bend to the left, then to the right again around a gravestone shop. Notice the old, wooden houses on the side street to the left as you pass, and on your route again on the right before you reach the next traffic light.

Take a right at the intersection, and a few steps ahead the road widens, then veers to the right. Shortly past the bend in the road on the right is **Makino Bros. & Co.**, a wholesaler of ivory carvings, where you can pick up a simple *netsuke*, the toggle used to balance the medicine or money purses over the belt worn with the kimono in the old days, for as little as ¥2,000. Ivory-carving is a dying craft in Japan, with only some 200 carvers still at work. Unlike other Asian countries, it's still done by hand here

National Museum of Western Art

55

and Makino acts as a middle-man between the carvers and retailers.

Follow the road back past the intersection where you turned right. A few steps on your right is **Taguchi Ningyoten**, makers of doll heads in an amazing variety. Taguchi-san takes orders from all over the country.

The first road on the right past Taguchi — quite long and narrow — leads past more temples with well-maintained gates and stone gardens. At the far end you'll spot the weather-worn, small vermilion gate of another temple, and just to the right of the gate is a fine, old wall made of mud and gray roof tiles.

Turn left facing the red gate and follow the narrow path around the temple to the right. At this point the road becomes a foot path too narrow for cars. Below the hill on the left you'll spot the Yanaka Community Center, a long, modern building. Follow the path on down the hill and around to the left. Just before you reach the next main road you'll see a narrow lane on the left of old, wooden houses with potted plants at the doors and the family bedding hanging out to dry.

Take a right onto the wide road ahead. This was the main street of the neighborhood in the old days. Past a children's playground on the right, you'll soon come to a fork in the road. Take a left, and within seconds you'll come to the entrance of **Yanaka Ginza**, this old neighborhood's equivalent of the more famous Ginza. The name aside, there is absolutely no resemblance. Enjoy what is a typical residential area shopping street full of the things ordinary people buy.

Back up a flight of steps, past a pet shop on the right, and onto the wide street leading to Nippori Station, you'll come to another gravestone shop on the right. Turn right

Yanaka

into this street, and not far on your left, set back off the street through a gate, you'll spot a sizeable concrete building. This is the **Asakura Sculpture Hall**, (¥250, 10 a.m. to 4:30 p.m., Sat., Sun. Mon.) named after a well-known, modern Japanese sculptor named Fumio Asakura. After seeing some of his works in the high-ceilinged studio on the main floor, be sure to climb the narrow steps from the second floor onto the roof garden, which affords a fine view of the paths you've tread, plus the sizeable **Yanaka Cemetery** which parallels the railroad tracks between Nippori and Uguisudani Stations.

UENO EATS & DRINKS

❶ **Horaiya** （蓬莱屋 上野3-28-5, Tel.831-5783）
A good *tonkatsu* (deep-fried pork cutlet) lunch for ¥2,000. 11:30 a.m. to 1:30 p.m.; 4:30-7 p.m., closed Mon.

❷ **Yabusoba** （籔蕎麦 湯島3-44-7, Tel.831-8977）
An old shop in a new but charming Japanese building serving buckwheat noodles nothing like **your** mother made. Considered one of Tokyo's three best Edo-style noodle shops. Try their *zarusoba*, cold noodles you dip in a soy sauce, during the summer months. Around ¥1,000. 11:30 a.m.-2 p.m.; 5-8 p.m., closed Wed.

❸ **Ponta** （ぽん多 上野3-23-3, Tel. 831-2351）
This place claims to have invented *tonkatsu* back in 1905. Also serves beef stew and fried shrimp. ¥1,500-¥2,000. 11 a.m. to 8 p.m., closed Mon.

❹ **Echikatsu** （江知勝 湯島2-31, Tel. 811-5293）
Sukiyaki in a walled-in private house and garden. This place was once frequented by Meiji-era writers Soseki Natsume and Ogai Mori. ¥5,000. 5-10 p.m., closed Sun., hol.

❺ **Tarumatsu** （たる松 上野6-8-10, Tel. 835-1755）
Japanese-style oyster stew, chicken stew and buttered scallops are the specialities, along with 15 kinds of sake. Behind Keisei Dept. ¥2,000-¥3,000. 4-11 p.m.

Tokyo National Museum

❻ Once Upon a Time　(上野1-3-3, Tel. 836-3799)

Booze, coffee and snacks — all a bargain by Tokyo standards — in a tiny red-brick 100-year-old sake brewery cluttered with knick-knacks. Shades of a Greenwich Village coffee house. Drinks, ¥500-¥600. Snacks, ¥500-¥700. 6-12 p.m., closed Sun., hol.

❼ Tensho　(天庄　湯島2-26-9, Tel. 837-6571)

Some of the best *tempura* in town is offered in this small restaurant on the street just behind Yushima Tenjin Shrine — and at prices you can afford: ¥800 for the special lunch *(teishoku)* (except Sun.) and ¥2,300 for the special dinner *(teishoku)*. 11:30 a.m.-1:30 p.m.; 5-11 p.m., closed Tues.

❽ Kikunoya　(喜久の家　湯島3-39-12, Tel. 831-5762)

Some Japanese gourmets insist Kansai food from the area around Osaka is better than Tokyo food, and this is an inexpensive place to find out for yourself. *Kakuni* (boiled pork), *sashimi* (raw fish) or *tempura teishoku* for ¥1,000; after 2 p.m., ¥1,200. 11:30 a.m.-11 p.m., closed Sun.

OFFBEAT UENO ATTRACTIONS

❾ Suzumoto Engeijo　(鈴本演芸場　上野2-7-12)

The last of the many story-telling theaters in this neighborhood. Monologues and dialogues designed to make the Japanese remember times past and snicker about the present. ¥1,700. 12:30-5; 5:30-9:30 p.m.

❿ Sento Tsubameyu　(銭湯燕湯　上野3-14-5)

Tokyo's only all-day public bath open from 6 a.m. to midnight, closed Mon. A morning bathers' association from the area gathers here for the opening each day. ¥230.

⓫ Yokoyama Taikan Memorial Hall

(横山大観記念館　池の端1-4-24, Tel. 821-1017)

This spacious home was once occupied the by late Yokoyama Taikan, one of Japan's most celebrated early 20th century artists, and it offers the best opportunity in the city to see how celebrities used to live, as well as a few of the artist's works. (¥300, 10 a.m.-4 p.m., closed Mon., Tues., Wed.)

⓬ Shitamachi Museum

(下町風俗資料館　上野公園2-1, Tel. 823-7461)

Here's your chance to see the combination shops/homes of Tokyo's downtown merchants before the great earthquake in 1923 and the fire bombings in 1945 — a recreated street lined with a sweet shop and a coppersmith's shop, and more. The handsome new building faces the south end of Shinobazu Pond. (¥200, 9:30 a.m.-4:30 p.m., closed Mon., hol.)

HARAJUKU-OMOTESANDO

Like Shinjuku, the Harajuku-Omotesando area is young and trendy. But surrounded by expensive residential areas where the Japanese elite and foreign diplomats rub elbows, it's quite probably the most international nook in all of Tokyo. This is where the boys and girls come to show off, and especially on Sunday when the wide Omotesando Dori adjacent to Harajuku Station becomes a pedestrian mall both through Yoyogi Park and on the tree-lined stretch leading from the station all the way down to the Omotesando intersection.

Young teen-agers from all over the city flock to Yoyogi Park on Sundays to dance in groups to recorded music their well-practiced routines. The majority are considered drop outs and would rather play than adhere to the country's rigid educational system. They leave their middle-class homes in regular rags, then later slip into satin pajama outfits or crinolines kept during the week in train station lockers.

Adjacent Meiji Shrine, one of Tokyo's most serene corners, stands in dramatic contrast to the fracas. This vast forest of trees and wide gravel paths is dedicated to the memory of the Emperor Meiji. The shrine buildings are imposing for their stark simplicity. Especially stunning are the iris beds in June, set apart in a separate garden.

Strolling down Omotesando, which Tokyoites call their "Champs Élysées", you'll notice a narrow lane veering slightly uphill on the left side of the street behind the La Foret Bldg. of boutiques before you reach the next main intersection. A few steps up the lane sits the **Ota Memorial Museum of Art** (¥500, 10:30 a.m. to 5:30 p.m. , closed Mon. & the last week of each month) of old woodblock prints.

Back on Omotesando, cross the busy intersection and continue along this wide avenue, allowing your fancies to run free in the very up-to-date shops and coffee parlors. Take a right at the second small street on the right after the intersection, and you'll find **Shimura's**, popular for its bamboo crafts, pottery and small gift items. **Kiddy Land**, as the names implies, is for kiddies — but some pretty sizeable ones. On weekends you can barely move through the aisles of novelties and toys.

Further down Omotesando, distinguished by its red shrine-like facade, is the **Oriental Bazaar**, another shop popular with foreign residents for a large selection of Imari ware, screens, old chests, lamp bases, plus the usual Oriental trinkets foreigners buy.

Just before the Omotesando intersection on the right you'll see a futuristic, mirrored palace dedicated to Japan's famous international dress designer **Hanae Mori**. The first floor offers her boutique items, haute couture on second and a basement full of both Oriental and western antiques.

The wide boulevard ends at Omotesando intersection, but the smart shops don't. Fashion, art and antique enthusiasts will want to continue into the narrow street on the other side of Aoyama Dori and straight ahead from Omotesando Dori. A five minute walk will bring you to perhaps the most sleekly elegant coffee shop in a city famous for such, known as **Yoku Moku**. There's an outdoor terrace for summertime sipping.

Further down the street in a red-brick commercial building are an **Issey Miyake boutique**, several men's and women's fashion shops and the cozy little French restaurant **Les Poisson Rouge**, where you can have a price-fixed lunch for ¥2,000. **Cafe Figaro** on the corner in the same building offers great cakes.

Continue on the street and just ahead on the other side of the next traffic signal you'll come to the **Nezu Institute of Fine Arts** (¥500, 9:30 a.m. to 4:30 p.m., closed Mon., Aug.), a private collection of Oriental art especially renowned for its Chinese bronzes and pottery and paintings connected with the tea ceremony. Don't miss the garden in the trees below. Tea ceremony instructions are given in the two tea houses, and this is a good place to find Japanese women in kimono.

Back at the traffic light outside the Nezu entrance gate turn left and walk to the next traffic light. On the left corner is **Matsushita & Associates**, one of the best wood-block print shops in Tokyo, where the selection is small but excellent. The street out front is lined with antique stores, most of them specializing in the ceramics so dearly loved by Japanese. The patient searcher might find something special here, but the price is not likely to be cheap.

This street takes you back to fashionable Aoyama Dori.

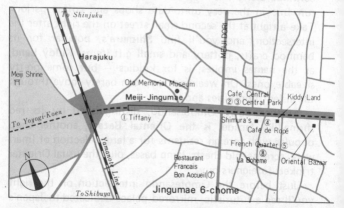

Turn right and in five minutes you'll reach Omotesando Station on the Ginza, Chiyoda and Hanzomon Lines of the subway.

HARAJUKU EATS & DRINKS

❶ Tiffany (ティファニー 神宮前4-30, Tel. 409-7777)
Faintly French, the usual snow peas and carrots on the side. Wide windows overlook the boulevard. ¥2,000-¥3,000. 11:30 a.m.-11 p.m.

❷ Cafe Central (カフェ・セントラル 神宮前4-30-6, Tel. 403-6557)
"Philippine Delicacy," the sign says, but a better handle is "garlic delicacy". Garlic haters beware. *Adobo, kari karing* and *pinak* are the specialties. ¥2,000 average. Room for 14 small bodies. Squeezed in a narrow alley beside Central Park (see below). 12-10 p.m., closed Sun.

❸ Central Park (セントラル・パーク 神宮前4-30-6, Tel.478-6200)
Drinks and snacks in a neon-ridden central courtyard of an apartment building. Pity the tenants. Open roof in the summer and palm trees the year round give it a New Orleans flavor. Always jammed with teeny-boppers. Less than ¥1,000. 11:30 a.m.-9 p.m.

❹ Café de Ropé (カフェ・ド・ロペ 神宮前6-1-9, Tel. 406-6845)
Sidewalk sipping and gawking. Drinks and snacks for less than ¥1,000. You'll almost think you're in Paris. 11 a.m.-9 p.m.

❺ French Quarter
(フレンチ・クォーター 神宮前5-10-10, Tel. 407-5184)
Italian food, despite the name, with entrees from ¥2,000 and fixed lunches for about ¥1,000. Cozy, European atmosphere. 11 a.m.-11 p.m.

❻ Sandwich House Bamboo
(バンブー 神宮前5-8-8, Tel. . 407-8427)
Tucked behind the Jubilee Plaza Bldg., this American-style cafeteria serves a variety of sandwiches, salads for under ¥1,000. 11 a.m.-9 p.m.

❼ Restaurant Français Bon Accueil
(ボン・アキュー 神宮前6-28-6, Tel. 498-4411)
Lunch, tea or dinner in a variety of handsomely appointed rooms with lunch courses from ¥1,000 and dinner from ¥4,000. The taste in Japanese-French. 11:30 a.m.-11 p.m.

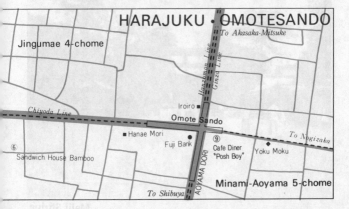

⑧ La Boheme (ラ・ボエーム 神宮前6-7-18, Tel. 400-3406)
Exotic spaghettis, coffee and cocktails in an attic-like setting filled with antiques. A great place for late-night noshing. Reached by the alley beside Café de Ropé. 12 noon-5 a.m.

⑨ Cafe Diner "Posh Boy"
(ポッシュ・ボーイ 南青山5-1-3, Tel. 406-8242)
6, 8 or 10 oz. hamburgers from ¥850-¥1,250 and pumpkin, almond or vegetable donuts for ¥150 are the specialties of this sleek, art nouveau diner popular with young city slickers. 2nd floor, la Mia shopping bldg. 11 a.m.-10 p.m.

INTERNATIONAL FLAVOR

When you're tired of going native — and even the hardiest Japanophile reaches that point occasionally — you have a choice of two swinging night life areas full of bars, clubs and restaurants more like the ones back home. The neighborhoods are Roppongi and Akasaka, and both are just a 10-minute subway ride from the Ginza.

Harajuku Street Dancer

Meiji Shrine

ROPPONGI EATS, DRINKS & MUSIC

❶ Almond （アマンド　六本木6-1-26, Tel. 402-1800）

This Roppongi landmark coffee shop just above the Roppongi subway station is a spot everyone knows — even Tokyo's generally unknowledgeable taxi drivers. Nothing inside especially recommendable, but convenient and almost always open. 9 a.m. – 6 a.m.

❷ Tong Fu （トンフー　六本木6-7-13, Tel. 403-3527）

Exotic cocktails and American-style Chinese food in a charming house done up in pre-war, decadent Shanghai atmosphere. Better for drinks than food, and there's an outside terrace in the summer. Drinks under ¥1,000. Dinner averages ¥2,000-¥3,000. 4 p.m.-2 a.m., closed Sun., hol.

❸ Mr. Stamp's
（ミスター・スタンプス　六本木4-4-2, Tel. 479-1390）

American Al Stamp serves American steaks for an average of ¥3,000, depending on the size, and offers French and American wine from the biggest cellar in Tokyo in an intimate room overlooking the Self Defence Headquarters. Just up the steps from Club Misty.

❹ Charleston （チャールストン　六本木3-8-11, Tel. 402-0372）

Western-style cocktails in a Casbah-like room with Victorian touches. The foreign swingers who hold sway here would be very much at home on New York's First Ave. A sign says "Private Club. Members Only," but foreign visitors are welcome. Down the hill from the B.S. Bldg. off the street leading to Tokyo Tower. Drinks average less than ¥1,000. 6 p.m.-6 a.m.

❺ Pub Cardinal
（パブカーディナル　六本木,六本木大昌ビル, Tel. 401-7855）

A *gaijin* (foreigner) meeting place which might persuade you to think you're not really so far from Dubuque. The mood is synthetic church. Stained glass and dim lights. Drinks less than ¥1,000. 5 p.m.-4 a.m.

❻ Roppoingi Pit Inn
（Roppongi ピットイン　六本木3-17-4, Tel. 585-1063）

Rock and jazz, and sometimes the big names turn up here. The performers change almost daily, so it's better to call and find out what's happening. ¥2,000 cover charge, plus drinks. From 7:30 p.m.

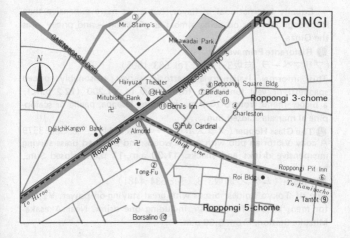

❼ Birdland (バードランド 六本木3-5, Tel. 478-3456)
One of Tokyo's top jazz spots, and it's the performers who are the draw, not the food or ambiance. ¥2,300 cover charge. The drinks are ¥800. In the sub-basement of the Roppongi Square Bldg.

❽ Roppongi Square Bldg. (六本木スクエアビル 六本木3-5)
Not a single disco, but a building with several. The names and popularity of these places change regularly, so it's best to just step inside each and discover the action for yourself. Roppongi discos average from ¥3,000-¥5,000 per person.

❾ A Tantôt
(ア・タント 六本木5-17-1アクシスビル3F, Tel. 586-4431)
Good French food, with bargain set lunches at less than ¥2,000, in a sleek room with an open kitchen and inlaid marble walls, plus a terrace for warm-weather dining. 3rd floor, Axis Bldg. (crammed with interior designers), down by Pit Inn. 11:30 a.m.-4 p.m.; 5:30-11 p.m., closed Mon.

❿ Borsalino (ボルサリーノ 六本木6-8-21, Tel. 401-7751)
A sophisticated Italian place in black and white which is several notches above the spaghetti and pizza Tokyo regulars. Not for bargain seekers, however. Dinners average ¥6,000 or ¥7,000 at night. Price-fixed lunches around ¥2,000. 12-5 p.m.; 6-11 p.m.; Sun., dinner only; closed Mon.

⓫ Berni Inn (バーニーイン 六本木3-13-14, Tel. 405-4928)
Another favorite with the foreign community who belly up to the bar for beer on tap. Reasonably-priced steaks in a separate room. Described as a "British Pub", but that stretches the imagination. 4 p.m.-2 a.m.; Sat., Sun. 12 p.m.-1 a.m. A separate Berni Inn for drinks only across from the Haiyuza Theater. Also in the Ginza, Shinjuku.

⓬ Hub (ハブ六本木店 六本木4-9-2, Tel. 478-0393)
Another "British pub", this one in the lobby of the Haiyuza Theater, a Japanese modern theater outpost (also art films every night at 10 p.m. — Tokyo's only late-night movie). Draft beer (¥200-¥450), whiskey (¥200-¥500) and snacks, with dart boards and stand-around tables. 10 a.m.-2 a.m.

AKASAKA EATS, DRINKS & MUSIC

Equally international in flavor, but a bit more expensive than Roppongi. Borders on being almost as glittering — and pricey — as the Ginza.

❶ Ristorante Primavera
(プリマベーラ 赤坂3-19-9, Tel. 583-1505)
This informal Italian-style *trattoria* serves reasonably priced spaghetti or veal lunch sets from ¥600 to ¥1,200 (12-2 p.m.); a bigger menu from 5-10 p.m., including lasagna, paella or scaloppine al marsala. Closed Sun.

❷ The Glass Hopper (グラスホッパー 赤坂3-11-7, Tel. 586-3579)
A cozy Victorian pub with warm woods and polished brass serving inexpensive drinks and snacks. 11:30 a.m.-11 p.m., closed Sun., hol.

❸ Mugen (ムゲン 赤坂3-8, Tel. 584-4481)
One of Tokyo's oldest discos with great staying-on power. ¥2,800 for men, ¥1,800 for women, including one drink. Near Akasaka-Mitsuke Station. From 6:30 p.m.

❹ Byblos (ビブロス 赤坂3-8, Tel. 584-4484)

Another disco old-timer — this one fussy about your dress. ¥2,000 for men, ¥1,000 for women, if you enter before 9 p.m. on week nights. After 9 p.m. and on weekends, ¥3,000 and ¥2,000. Includes two drinks. Near Akasaka-Mitsuke Station. From 7 p.m.

❺ Suntory The Cellar

(サントリー館 赤坂2-14-3, Tel. 470-1131)

On the main floor of the Suntory Bldg. across the street and under the expressway from Akasaka Mitsuke Station. Beer, whiskey and snacks in a Mediterranean atmosphere. 5-11 p.m., closed Sun., hol.

❻ Anna Miller's (アンナミラーズ 赤坂3-4, Tel. 586-7369)

"Kissin' wears out, cookin' don't" says the sign — and what could be more Japanese than that? American-style sandwiches, chili, quiche, good salads — and the best pies in Tokyo in this Tokyo version of a California-based chain of Pennsylvania Dutch coffee shops. 7:30 a.m.-9:30 p.m. Also on Aoyama Dori, in Harajuku, Meguro, Jiyugaoka, Komazawa, Hiroo.

❼ Shabu Gen (しゃぶ玄 赤坂3-8-1, Tel. 586-4054)

Inexpensive *shabu shabu* — meat, fish and vegetables you boil yourself — on the 5th floor of the Aruto Bldg. just beside Akasaka-Mitsuke Station. A "Shabu-Gen Dinner" for ¥2,500, or "Special Dinner" for ¥3,500. 11:30 a.m.-2:30 p.m.; 5-11 p.m. Sun. and hol. — dinner only.

❽ Stonefield's

(ストーンフィールド 赤坂3-21-4, Tel. 583-5690)

Sam. Ishihara, country singer-song writer, dishes up bourbon, corn-on-the-cob and country potatoes in this "Nostalgic American Country Music Saloon" featuring country western recordings and an occasional live entertainer. 6 p.m.-1 a.m., closed Sun., hol.

❾ Mexico Cafe y Arte

(メキシコ・カフェ・イ・アルテ 赤坂4-1-2, Tel. 586-0268)

Expresso, tequila and diet cake amid Mexican costumes and folk art, all for sale. 12-10 p.m., closed Sun., hol.

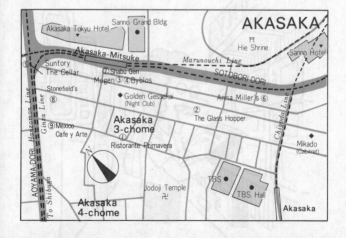

SHOPPING OFF THE TOURIST TRAIL

Akihabara, just two stops north of Tokyo Station on the Yamanote Line, is a must for stereo, video and electronics gadget freaks. Prices are 20 to 30 per cent less than the rest of the city, and the big stores have tax-free sections where the equipment is made for the volts and cycles back home.

Ameya Yokocho beside Okachimachi Station, one stop north of Akihabara on the JNR Yamanote Line, is for imported jewelry, handbags, lighters and pens, all piled high in the many tiny shops beneath the tracks. The well-traveled insist that prices for this type of luxury goods are cheaper here than even Hong Kong, and the dealers more reliable.

Flea Markets are held once a week at various locations: Arai Yakushi Temple (Arai Yakushi-mae Station, Seibu Shinjuku Line) and Togo Shrine (Harajuku Station, JNR Yamanote Line or Meiji Jingumae Station, Chiyoda Line) on the first Sunday of every month; Nogi Shrine (Nogizaka Station, Chiyoda Line) on the second Sunday; Sunshine City's Alpa shopping arcade B1 (Ikebukuro Station, JNR Yamanote Line, Marunouchi Line, Yurakucho Line) on the third Saturday and Sunday; and again at Togo Shrine on the fourth Sunday. Good places to pick up old fabrics, a second-hand abacus, china, chests.

Kanda around Jimbocho Station (Mita Line, Shinjuku Line) is packed with tiny bookshops, many of them specializing in particular subjects and practically all of them with at least a few English-language books. Kitazawa and Isseido are especially good for used books on Japan and Asia. Yamada, across the street from Isseido, has a nice selection of both old and modern prints. Further up the street is Ohya Shobo, with a large selection of old prints, books and maps. the Tokyo Komingu Kotto-Kan around the next corner features five floors of curios.

Kokusai Kankō Kaikan, just outside the north entrance of Tokyo Station on the Yaesu side, houses the Tokyo promotional offices of the prefectural governments, each with its own products for sale, mostly handicrafts and food items.

MUSEUMS FOR THE SPECIALIST

Japan Folk Crafts Museum (Komaba Todai-mae Station, Inokashira Line — just two stops from Shibuya). A must for the Japanese folk craft enthusiast. This was once the home of Yanagi Soetsu, the man who got the Japanese back on the folk art trail, and the building alone is a treasure. (¥500, open 10 a.m. to 5 p.m., closed Mon.)

Paper Museum (Oji Station, JNR Keihin Line). This is the world's largest museum of paper, with a special section on the manufacture of traditional Japanese *washi*. (Free, open 9:30 a.m. to 4:30 p.m. closed Mon.)

Idemitsu Art Gallery (Yurakucho Station, JNR Yamanote Line) Located on the ninth floor of the Kokusai Bldg., Marunouchi, this museum is a must for ceramics fans, also Oriental bronzes, calligraphy and paintings. (¥500, open 10 a.m. to 5 p.m., closed Mon.)

Hatakeyama Memorial Gallery (Takanawadai Station, Toei Ichigo Line) Every accouterment for the tea ceremony, Japan's great inspiration for the arts. (¥500, open 10 a.m. to 4:30, closed Mon.)

Sword Museum (Sangubashi Station, Odakyu Line) A good introduction to Japan's fine art of swordmaking, with 30 "National Treasures". (¥500, open 9 a.m. to 4 p.m., closed Mon.)

Museum of Maritime Science (船の科学館) (reached by ferry from Takeshiba Pier) Replicas and visuals of the shipping industry in a concrete building shaped like a steamship out in Tokyo Bay. (¥500, 10 a.m. to 5 p.m. daily.)

Meiji University Criminal Museum (Ochanomizu Station, JNR Chuo or Sobu Lines) on the third floor, Ogawamachi School Bldg. Criminal-capturing tools from the Edo period, plus old documents. (Free, 10 a.m. to 4:30 p.m., closed Sat. afternoon, Sun.)

Tokyo Craftsman

TOKYO DAY TRIPS

Tokyo is smack in the middle of a host of scenic and historic sights which can be reached within a few hours. Possibilities include:

Kamakura, administrative center of the military government in the 12th and 13th centuries, still has enough old temples and shrines, as well as classic Japanese homes with thatched-roofed gates to make you forget the present. Highly recommended is a walk behind **Kenchoji Temple** through a small valley and up the steps to another small temple, from where you catch a trail over the tree-studded hills and down the other side into a residential street that leads to **Kamakura-gu Shrine**. The hike takes about one hour. Have a Japanese-style taco at the coffee shop Bon across the street. Then stroll back through the residential lanes to **Tsurugaoka Hachimangu Shrine**, dedicated to the war god which no doubt helped put the town's military Minamoto clan in the driver's seat. You can stroll to Kamakura Station through the park in the center of the wide boulevard leading to the Shrine, or a narrow, shopping street paralleling the main road to the right. Three stops from Kamakura Station on the old-fashioned Enoshima-Kamakura Kanko Line is Hase Station, from where it's a 10-minute walk to the famous **Great Buddha** which sits outside in the open air. To reach Kita-Kamakura, take the JNR Yokosuka Line from Tokyo, Shimbashi or Shinagawa Stations (¥640, 1 hour).

Great Buddha

68

Hakone, in the mountains between the city and Mt. Fuji, is a spectacularly scenic resort area with many hot springs, hiking trails, small museums and views of the famous mountain. Take the Odakyu "Romance Car" from Shinjuku to Hakone-Yumoto at the foot of the mountains (¥1,160, 1 hour 50 minutes). At Yumoto switch to the Hakone Tozan Railway, a cute, little two-car tram that zig-zags up the mountains all the way to Gora (¥270, 45 minutes), from where you can take a cable car to Sounzan (¥280) and then a ropeway to Togendai (¥920) on the north shore of Lake Ashi. Before Gora you can stop off at **Chokoku-no-mori** to see the **Hakone Open Air Museum** of sculpture, or one stop before at **Kowakidani** for a 10-minute hike to Chisuji-no-taki waterfall, then on to a hiking trail which will bring you back down to the next town below — Miyanoshita (allow about two hours). From Miyanoshita, you can catch the train back down to **Hakone-Yumoto.**

Nikko

Nikko is both a shrine dedicated to the first Tokugawa *Shogun* Ieyasu and a scenic wonderland of mountains and lakes. The foliage is especially beautiful in mid-October. **Toshogu Shrine**, plastered with gold and polychrome, is less a reflection of traditional Japanese taste than the megalomania of the Tokugawas. But feast your eyes on the very ancient cedar trees that surround it and, if possible, take a hike up into those forests, right on par with those in the film "Rashomon". From the Nishi Sando bus stop near the shrine it's about a 50-minute ride by Tobu Bus (¥650) to **Chuzenji Lake** and nearby **Kegon Waterfall**. You can reach Nikko town by the private Tobu Line "Romance Car" from Asakusa Station (¥1,840, 1 hour 45 minutes).

Chichibu is both a town and a National Park (Chichibu-Tama) northwest of Tokyo, and about as close to the wilderness as you can get in the city environs. Half the fun of this unspoiled area is getting there. First you take the Seibu-Ikebukuro Line's "Red Arrow Romance Car" from Ikebukuro to Chichibu (¥970). At Chichibu Seibu Station take a left outside the station, follow the footpath along the tracks, cross the tracks and take a right to the dilapidated Ohanabatake Station. Catch the next train on the Chichibu Line bound for Mitsumine Guchi (¥230), last stop. Then hop on to a waiting Seibu Bus to Chichibuko Station (¥300). Then take a waiting yellow microbus up the mountain two stops to Hayashidaira. Just below the bus stop is **Kobushi Minshuku**, (Tel. (04945) 5-0457) a former old farm house where you can hibernate far from the maddening crowds. Down the hill and across the river on a rickety foot bridge a path leads to Fudotaki Waterfall, so pristine you'll think you're in Borneo, not Japan. Allow about four hours from Ikebukuro.

Mt. Fuji, the granddaddy of Japanese peaks at 12,388 ft., can be climbed from July 1-August 31. But don't expect to have the trail to yourself. You'll be eating the dust of the person ahead of you all the way. There are five climbing trails to choose from, with Kawaguchiko being the most popular and accessible from Tokyo. Buses are available from Tokyo's Hamamatsucho Station (¥2,000) and Shinjuku Station (¥1,850) direct to the fifth stage of the trail daily from July 10-August 31, and on Sundays only from the third Sun. in April-third Sun. in November. Allow about 2 hours 30 minutes. From the fifth stage it's about a five-hour climb to the summit. Some start climbing in early afternoon and reach the eighth stage before dark to lodge in a hut. Then they climb the rest of the way in the morning. Others prefer starting in late afternoon and climbing all night to see the sunrise from the summit. The descent is usually made on the Subashiri Trail leaving the summit in the morning and arriving at the fifth stage in late afternoon. From the fifth stage, take a bus to Gotemba (¥800), then a direct JNR Asagiri train to Shinjuku (¥2,300). You can make a reservation on the direct bus to the Kawaguchiko fifth stage through a travel agent or with Fuji Kyuko Railway (Tel. 352-5487).

TOKYO SLEEPING

BUSINESS HOTELS

These are your best bet in Tokyo where convenience is worth a little extra money. *Minshuku* there are, but none are located near the center. The following were selected with an eye to proximity to a major JNR or subway station and generally low prices.

Ginza Capital Hotel, Tsukiji 3-chome, Chuo-ku, 543-8211. Two minutes from Tsukiji Station on the Hibiya Line, reasonable walk to Ginza. Singles from ¥5,560, twins from ¥8,800.

Hokke Club Ikenohata, Ikenohata 2-chome, Taito-ku, 822-3111. Five minutes from Yushima Station on the Chiyoda Line subway. Convenient to Ueno Park, Nippori area and Tokyo University. Singles, ¥4,000, twins from ¥7,400.

Akasaka Shampia Hotel, Akasaka 7-chome, Minato-ku, 586-0811. Seven minutes from Akasaka Station on the Chiyoda Line subway. Handy to Akasaka and Roppongi, popular night spots. Singles ¥5,500, twins ¥8,800.

Keiunso Shinkan, Yoyogi 2-chome, Shibuya-ku, 370-0333. Three minutes from Shinjuku Station. Convenient to Shinjuku and Shibuya area. Japanese style — just 13 rooms. ¥4,400 per person.

Mikawaya Bekkan, Asakusa 1-chome, Taito-ku, 843-2345. Three minutes from Asakusa Station on the Ginza Line. Close to Asakusa's pleasures. ¥4,500 per person, with breakfast. Japanese style.

Toko Hotel, Nishi Gotanda 2-chome, Shinagawa-ku, 494-1050. Not in the center, but right beside Gotanda Station on the JNR Yamanote Line and 20 minutes to the Ginza or Shinjuku. Singles ¥5,700, twins from ¥9,600.

Tokyo YWCA Sadohara Hotel (women only), Ichigaya Sadohara-cho 3-chome, Shinjuku-ku, 268-7313. Three minutes from Ichigaya Station on the JNR Sobu Line, Tozai and Yurakucho Lines of the subway. Close to Yasukuni Shrine, Kitanomaru Park. Singles from ¥4,300, twins ¥8,600.

Tokyo YMCA (men only), Kanda Mitoshirocho 7-chome, Chiyoda-ku, 293-1911. Ten minutes from the JNR Kanda Station, five minutes from Awajicho Station on the Marunouchi Line. Near the Kanda second-hand book stores and several universities, not far by subway or train to the Ginza. Singles from ¥4,200, twins from ¥7,400.

Asia Center of Japan, Akasaka 8-chome, Minato-ku, 402-6111. Six minutes from Aoyama-Itchome Station on the Ginza Line subway. Convenient to Aoyama Dori, Akasaka and Roppongi. Singles from ¥3,500 up, twins from ¥4,800 up.

Diamond Hotel, 25 Ichiban-cho, Chiyoda-ku, 231-2764. Five minutes from Kojimachi Station on the Yurakucho Line by which it's a 10-minute ride to the Ginza, 20-minutes to Ikebukuro. In a quiet residential area behind the British Embassy and near the

Imperial Palace. Singles from ¥5,000, twins from ¥8,500.

Shinagawa Prince Hotel, 4-10-30 Takanawa, Minato-ku 440-1111. Across the street from Shinagawa Station on the Yamanote Line, this big (1,020 rooms) hotel sits on top of a complete sports complex. Singles from ¥6,100. A budget member of a big chain.

Shibuya Tokyu Inn, 1-24-10 Shibuya, Shibuya-ku, 498-0109. Steps from Shibuya Station, a commuter changing point, surrounded by spots catering to Tokyo's youth. Convenient by train to all of the city. Singles ¥7,200, doubles ¥9,400.

Hotel Kayu Kaikan, 8-1 Sanban-cho, Chiyoda-ku, 230-1111. Ten minutes from Kudanshita Station, near Chidorigafuchi Park. The Hotel Okura's fine food and service at about half the cost. In quiet residential area, and a good value for the money. Singles ¥8,200, doubles ¥11,500-¥15,500.

Harajuku Trim, 6-28-6 Jingumae, Shibuya-ku, 498-2101. In an office building near Harajuku Station on the Yamanote Line; Jingumae Station on the Chiyoda Line. Trendy Harajuku area. Great for jocks, as they can use in-house club facilities for ¥800. Singles ¥5,500, twins ¥9,000.

Gajoen Kanko Hotel, 1-8-1 Shimo Meguro, Meguro-ku, 491-0111. Five minutes from Meguro Station on the Yamanote Line, from which it's a 15-minute ride to Shinjuku, 20 minutes to Tokyo Station. The perfect spot for Japanese art nouveau lovers. Don't let the lobby fool you. Behind it is a treasure of pre World War II interior detail. In a quiet residential area. Singles ¥5,800, twins ¥7,300.

The President Hotel, 2-2-3 Minami Aoyama, Minato-ku, 242-2307. Brand new and in a top location beside Aoyama Itchome Station on the Ginza Line, near smart shops and restaurants. Lobby offers hints of Europe, though in plastic replica. Single ¥6,300 up, twins ¥12,000 up.

Hilltop Hotel (Yamanoue Hotel), 1-1 Surugadai, Kanda, Chiyoda-ku, 293-2311. Pricey in comparison with the others in this listing, but a good buy for the money, if you like well-restored old buildings and a quiet location. Five minutes from Ochanomizu Station on the Chuo and Sobu Lines, close to Kanda's book stores, universities. Nice restaurants and a summertime outdoor beer garden sheltered by trees. Singles ¥9,000 up, twins ¥14,000 up.

Hotel Tokyo, 2-17-8 Takanawa, Minato-ku, 447-5771. Quiet, family style hotel featuring western rooms with Japanese touches such as tatami area and wooden baths. Just above Senkakuji Station on the Toei-Asakusa Line. Singles ¥8,800, twins ¥12,000 up.

Shiba Yayoi Convention Hall, 10-27, Kaigan 1-chome, Minato-ku, 434-6841. New, with great views from Takeshiba Pier location over the harbor and Hama Rikyu Park. Seven minutes from Hamamatsucho Station on the Yamanote Line. Singles ¥4,700, twins ¥6,900.

YOUTH HOSTEL

Ichigaya Youth Hostel, 1-6 Gobancho, Chiyoda-ku, 262-5950. Near Ichigaya Station. Reasonably close to the universities around Kanda, a short train ride to Shinjuku. ¥1,150 per person.

HAKONE SLEEPING

Matsuzakaya, 64 Motohakone, Hakone-machi, Ashigarashimo-gun, Kanagawa Pref., (0460) 3-6315. A Japanese-style inn with 20 rooms. A 50-minute bus ride from Odawara Station. ¥3,000-¥4,000 per person without meals. ¥8,000-¥10,000 per person with two meals. No singles.

Suikokan, 1300-402 Gora, Hakone-machi, Kanagawa, (0462)2-6315. A Japanese inn way up in Gora, and just a two-minute walk from the Hakone Tozan railway station. ¥7,000-¥10,000 price range.

NIKKO SLEEPING

Nikko Green Hotel, 9-19 Honmachi, Nikko, Tochigi Pref., (0288)54-1756. Japanese style, with two western-style rooms. ¥4,000-¥7,000 price range with two meals.

Lodge Sanboa, 1560 Tokorono, Nikko, Tochigi Pref., (0288) 53-3399. Small western-style hotel with rooms for two, four or six people only. A 15-minute walk from Nikko Station. ¥4,000-¥7,000 price range.

LAKE KAWAGUCHI (MT. FUJI) SLEEPING

Fuji-so, 735, Kodachi, Kawaguchiko-machi, Minamitsuru-gun, Yamanashi Pref., (05557) 2-1869. A *minshuku* in this scenic, lake-side resort town. Standard *minshuku* rates.

Onsen bath

KYOTO

京都

KYOTO: TRADITIONAL JAPANESE TASTE

As in Tokyo, your first stop should be the JNTO **TIC** office, right across the street from Kyoto Station in the Kyoto Tower Bldg. (Tel. 371-5649), same hours as Tokyo. The staff will give you good maps of the city with bus routes and help you find a place to stay.

Around the station you're apt to think Kyoto is just one more Japanese big city. To get a feeling for the old capital, quiet strolls either alone or with a thoughtful friend are recommended, and especially in the areas where we've outlined walks. Other spots where you can tune in on this city's special mood will be listed separately.

Kyoto was home to the Japanese Emperors and their retinue of courtiers, and Buddhist monks from its founding in 794 A.D. when Tang Dynasty influence from China was strong until 1868 when the Emperor Meiji settled in Tokyo.

The Buddhist monks remained, and Kyoto is still headquarters for many of the major Japanese Buddhist sects. The situation gives an unmistakable solemnity to the city. It makes you want to tip-toe and speak in whispers.

There is no better place to contemplate true Japanese taste: both its spare aspects influenced by Zen Buddhism and the tea ceremony and its love for gorgeous decoration. Like few other cities in the world, there is something to stir the mind and heart around every corner.

That so much remains from the past is due partly to the fact that unlike Tokyo people, Kyoto people take pride in old things; and partly to the fact that Kyoto was not damaged in World War II. The temple buildings may not be the originals, for this city has, after all, had a long and often violent history. But if not, they have been painstakingly recreated, some of them many times.

HIGASHIYAMA

The Higashiyama (East Mountain) area offers all that makes Kyoto a gorgeous old gal in capsule form. Start at **Ginkakuji** (Silver Pavilion), a 15-minute bus or taxi ride from the center. Now a Buddhist temple, this was once the country villa of Ashikaga Yoshimasu, the eighth of the Ashikaga *Shoguns*, who retired here in 1483. It was patterned after the more famous **Kinkakuji** (Gold Pavilion) on the other side of town which was built by Yoshimasu's grandfather, Yoshimitsu, though Kinkakuji is now a replica since the original was burned down by an arson in the 1950s. Ginkakuji survives as the only original structure from the period. It was never covered in silver leaf as intended, but it is a fine example of the kind of reserved elegance enjoyed by the wealthy of the time. The garden is equally famous for its combination of fine rocks and varieties of moss, and you can almost imagine Yoshimasu ambling down the paths in silk kimono.

From Ginkakuji stroll back down the street lined with souvenir shops to a canal bordered by cherry trees and turn left to meander along the gravel **"Philosopher's Walk"**,

Ginkakuji Temple

KYOTO

Nishijin Ori Kaikan

Jofukuji Temple

Daichi ⑩

IMADEGAWA DORI ⑨
Nashinoki Inn

Omiya Gosho

Old Imperial Palace

MARUTAMACHI DORI

Tomatsuya ㉑

Nijo Castle

Kyoto Business Hotel

OIKE DORI

Heian Museum

(Public Bath) Sakurayu

Rokkakudori

Nishiki-no-Ichiba
Tanakaya ⑰ ㉓ Tachikichi ⑬

Erizen Kyo ③

SHIJO DORI

Ōmiya   Karasuma   Kawara-machi

Takashimaya Dept.

Inabayakushi Temple

Hankyu Dept.

Mibudera Temple

Kandaijin Shrine

Bukkoji Temple

GOJO DORI

Tanba-
guchi

Costume Museum

Shosei-en Garden

Nishi-Honganji Temple

Higashi-Honganji Temple

Ryokan ⑧
Hiraiwa

SHICHIJO DORI ④ Kyoto Tower Hotel   Shichijo

① Hokke Club Kyoto
Kyoto Tower

San-in Main Line

Kyoto

To Shin-Osaka

To Arashiyama

Shijo-Omiya

SENBON DORI

HORIKAWA DORI

KARASUMA DORI

TERAMACHI DORI

KAWARAMACHI DORI

San-in Main Line

Nijō

To Saga

SHIJO DORI

Kintetsu Kyoto Line

Tōji

KUJO DORI

Toji Temple

To Kintetsu Nara

Nara Line

Tofukuji

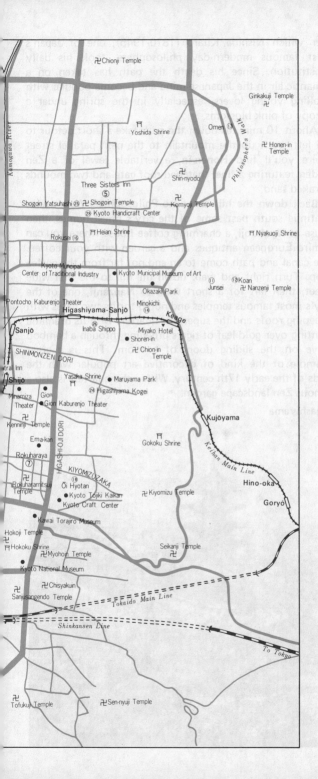

over which Nishida Kitaro (1870-1945), one of Japan's most famous modern-day philosophers, took his daily constitution. Since his death the path has taken on a romantic air in the Japanese mind and become popular with strolling young lovers, especially in the spring under a canopy of pink blossoms.

About 10 minutes down the path take a short detour to the left, back up the mountain to the next parallel street where you'll find **Honen-in**, a veritable jewel of a Zen garden featuring a fine, thatched-roof gate and two mounds of raked sand.

Back down the hill and onto Philosopher's Walk again, continue south past some of the city's finest homes, then pause at **Nyakuoji**, a charming coffee house where you can admire European antiques and a garden with your coffee. The canal and path come to an end not far from the coffee shop. Turn right and walk down the hill to the first wide street, then left for a short walk to **Nanzenji**, one of the city's most famous temples and noted for its two gates with sweeping roofs and the superior's quarters with its dramatic painting over gold leaf of tigers prowling through a bamboo grove on the sliding doors of a room. This is a great example of the kind of decorative art popular with the lords of the early 17th century. Within the quarters is also a famous Zen landscape garden.

Higashiyama

KIYOMIZU-GION

Kiyomizu, perched on the mountainside southeast of the business district, is everybody's favorite temple. What pleases are the way the wooden buildings blend with the natural surroundings, including cherry trees in the spring and maples in the fall, and the wide view of Kyoto from the terrace.

Walk down the steep, narrow street that leads to the temple with shops featuring Kyoto's own Kiyomizu pottery. At a fork in the road a flight of stone steps leads down to the right. From here the granite-paved, narrow streets and alleyways wind past small shops, mud and straw walls and thatched gates — all right out of a samurai movie.

You can amble through this area all the way to **Maruyama Park**, another famous cherry blossom place, and the adjacent **Chion-in**, headquarters for the popular Jodo sect of Buddhism. The temple's gate is considered the most imposing in all Japan, and the gigantic bell in the belfry is one of several which officially ring in the New Year.

Below Maruyama Park and across Higashiyama St. lies **Gion**, Japan's ultimate geisha quarter, where some of the country's most celebrated geisha still entertain those who can afford it. The quarter is especially noted for its *maiko*, or apprentice geisha, distinguished by their youth and the longer length of their kimono sleeves.

A stroll through Gion, especially after dark, can be rewarding. It's low on neon and high on soft light through paper windows, and if you're lucky, a *maiko* may just slip out from a sliding door and pass you on her way to work. With a high wig and her face painted white, she's living proof that this old tradition hasn't completely been abandoned for the girls in the Ginza.

Gion Quarter

Song and dance performances by Gion geisha for foreigners are held twice daily at the Gion Corner Yasaka Kaikan Hall, a section of the Gion Kaburenjo Theater, Mar.-Nov., 8 and 9:10 p.m. (¥1,800). Perhaps even more enchanting than Gion is **Pontocho**, a narrow alley lined with places where Geisha entertain, parallel to the Kamo River along the west bank between Shijo and Sanjo Sts.

ARASHIYAMA

This area west of Kyoto, where the Hozu River flows out of the mountains, has been a favorite spot for an outing since the beginning of Kyoto's history. The chief attraction is the scenery — gentle hills covered with cherry, maple and bamboo — and the river itself. There are buses from the city, but the fastest way is to catch the Keifuku Electric Railway from Shijo Omiya Station to the terminal at Arashiyama (¥170), or the Hankyu Railway from Kawaramachi Station to the Hankyu Arashiyama Station (¥140), changing trains at Katsura. From either station it's a short walk to the river, where you can hire a boat for a lazy cruise. Then walk back past the Keifuku Station and to the left to **Tenryuji**, another villa turned into a temple, this one once belonging to an emperor. If it's lunch time, treat yourself to a rare experience at **Sagano**, a restaurant specializing in hot bean curd *(yudofu)*, just south of the Tenryuji main entrance. The ¥2,000 lunch is served in a bamboo grove.

Arashiyama

Stick to the paths closest to the hills and walk north from Tenryuji. You'll pass a number of Buddhist temples and Shinto shrines which blend into their surroundings so well, it's easy to miss them. Never mind. The lush bamboo forests alone are worth the trip out from town.

ZEN GARDENS, PALACES

Outside the special areas above, Kyoto's sights are widely scattered across the wide plain between the mountains which surrounded the city on all sides but the south. The attractions fall into two broad types — more temples, either famous for their Zen gardens or some gorgeously decorated room, often brought intact from a former palace; or several palaces and castles.

Two musts for rock garden enthusiasts are Ryoanji and Daitokuji. **Ryoanji** is the one you've seen pictures of — just 15 rocks in various shapes and sizes strategically placed in a long, rectangle of raked gravel. Get here no later than 8 a.m. before the tour buses arrive, or forget it. Zen students have been pondering the meaning of this garden since its completion at the early part of the 16th century. The pond below, which reflects the verdant hills above, dates from quite early in the city's history and was also once part of a villa.

Daitokuji, east of the hills where Ryoanji and Kinkakuji lie, is not a single temple but a monastery of sub-temples, about a half dozen of which feature famous Zen gardens: Daisen-in, Koto-in and Ryogen-in are especially nice. These small sub-temples were built by prominent lords who favored the place during the 16th century. Also notice the

Daitokuji Temple

several gates, especially the big, red Chinese gate, brought here from the 16th century war lord Hideyoshi's fabulous Fushimi Castle (parts of which are all over Kyoto); and the two-story gate, attributed to Sen-no-Rikyu, who got the Japanese on the tea ceremony trail.

Among the castles and palaces, everyone wants to see **Nijo Castle** (¥400, 8:45 a.m.-4 p.m.), originally the Kyoto home of the first Tokugawa Shogun Ieyasu. It was taken over by the Imperial Household after the Meiji Restoration and has been altered considerably over the years, the Tokugawa crest replaced by the Imperial crest wherever possible. There are greater works of art at other palaces, but this gives an overall view of life in a Kyoto palace, complete with corridor floors made of wood that creaks at the lightest footfall — a way to warn the *shogun* of impending danger.

At **Nishi-Honganji Temple** near Kyoto Station you can view a few of the rooms from Hideyoshi's Fushimi Castle. This is probably the finest place in the city to see how the rooms of the rich looked during the Momoyama period, noted for its color and decoration. There are no English tours, but you can join one of the Japanese tours which are scheduled throughout the day. Although somewhat faded, the paintings over gold on the sliding doors and ceilings, plus two Noh stages, offer touches of gilded genius.

For admission to the **Old Imperial Palace** and the two **Imperial Villas, Katsura and Shugaku-in**, you must get permission from the Imperial Household Agency at the Old Imperial Palace. The two villas require reservations by phone ((075)211-1211) at least two days in advance (five days in advance during April-May, October-November) and

Nijo Castle

82

filling out forms at the office a day in advance. Don't forget your passport. At the Old Imperial Palace you can join an escorted 50-minute English tour at 10 a.m. and 2 p.m. on weekdays, 10 a.m. on Saturday mornings, by registering at least 20 minutes in advance. Passport necessary. Katsura Villa is most reflective of classic Japanese taste and should be your choice if time is limited.

KYOTO SLEEPING

❶ Hokke Club Kyoto （法華クラブ京都）
Kyoto Ekimae, Shimogyo-ku, (075) 361-1251. Just outside the Karasuma exit of Kyoto Station. Singles ¥5,050 up, twins ¥8,200 up.

❷ Kyoto Business Hotel （京都ビジネスホテル）
Kiyamachi-Oike-Agaru, Nakagyo-ku, (075) 222-1220. 10 minutes from Kyoto Station by bus. Singles ¥4,000 up, twins ¥6,000 up.

❸ Kyoto Central Inn （京都セントラルイン）
Shijo-Kawaramachi Nishi, Shimogyo-ku, (075) 211-8494. Recently renovated. Conveniently located near shopping center and equal distances to surrounding attractions. Singles ¥4,700 up, twins ¥8,000 up.

❹ Kyoto Tower Hotel （京都タワーホテル）
Kyoto Ekimae, Shimogyo-ku, (075) 361-3211. Handy location right in front of Kyoto Station. Singles ¥6,900 up, twins ¥10,500 up.

❺ Three Sisters Inn (Rakuto-so) （洛東荘）
Okazaki-michi, Kurodani-mae, Sakyo-ku, (075) 761-6336. Japanese rooms, with a few western additions to the joy of the predominantly foreign clientele. English-speaking staff can help you find your way around the city. Nearby annex has bath in every room. Singles ¥6,900 up, twins ¥10,800 up with breakfast (no bath).

❻ Myokenji （妙顕寺）
Horikawa-Teranouchi, Kamigyo-ku, (075) 414-0808. A Buddhist temple *minshuku* convenient to Daitokuji and Ryoanji. ¥3,500 with breakfast.

❼ Rokuharaya Inn （六波羅屋）
147 Takemura-cho, Higashiyama-ku, (075) 531-2776. Old-style inn in charming Gion quarter, handy to Kiyomizudera and Higashiyama attractions. Singles ¥4,000 per person with two meals, ¥3,500 with breakfast only, ¥3,000 with no meals.

❽ Ryokan Hiraiwa （平岩）
314 Hayao-cho, Kaminoguchi-agaru, Ninomiyacho-dori, Shimogyo-ku, (075) 351-6748. Another cozy inn popular with foreigners and a short bus ride from Kyoto Station. ¥2,500, without meals.

❾ Nashinoki Inn （梨の木）
Teramachi-nishi-iru, Imadegawa, Kamigyo-ku, (075) 241-1543. Convenient to Old Imperial Palace and reasonable distance to Higashiyama, Daitokuji or central business district. ¥4,000 without meals, ¥4,400 with breakfast, ¥7,000 with two meals.

KYOTO EATS & DRINKS

❿ Daichi
（大市 上京区下長者町通千本西上ル, Tel. (075)461-1775）
Snapping turtle (*suppon*) is the specialty, either marinated in sake and boiled in a pot, or in a thick soup with rice gruel and an egg.

¥15,000 up. 12:30 to 8 p.m., closed Tues.

⓫ Junsei（順正 左京区南禅寺草川町60, Tel.(075)761-2311）
One of a number of restaurants serving *yudofu* (boiled bean curd) and vegetarian dishes near Nanzenji Temple, but this is one of the oldest dating from 1834. ¥2,000 up. 11 a.m.-8 p.m.

⓬ Koan（壺庵 左京区南禅寺福地町33, Tel.(075)771-2781）
Vegetarian delicacies in a temple atmosphere with a garden, including noodles made from soy bean flour. ¥2,500. Lunch only. 10 a.m.-4:30 p.m., closed Wed.

⓭ Omen（おめん 左京区浄土寺石橋町74, Tel.(075)771-8994）
Good noodles near Ginkakuji Temple in Higashiyama for from ¥700. 11 a.m.-11 p.m., closed Thurs.

⓮ Minokichi（美濃吉 左京区粟田口鳥居町65, Tel.(075)771-4185）
Famous and old (1716), serves *kaiseki ryori*, a Kyoto specialty of fish and vegetables in their natural state served in lovely lacquer ware. ¥3,000 up. 11:30 a.m.-9 p.m.

⓯ Shimogamo Saryo

（下鴨茶寮 左京区下鴨泉川町, Tel.(075)701-5185）
More *kaiseki* — they call their lunch special *junsei bento* — in a room full of folk art. ¥2,000 11 a.m.-9 p.m.

⓰ Rokusei（六盛 左京区岡崎天王町60, Tel.(075)751-6171）
A famous restaurant near Heian Shrine with more *kaiseki*, this time served in a nice, basket-shaped serving dish known as *teoke bento*. ¥1,800 up. 11:30-8 p.m.

KYOTO SHOPPING

The main shopping drag is **Kawaramachi Dori** between Shijo and Oike Dori, along with two covered shopping arcades that parallel Kawaramachi to the west. Shops selling Kyoto specialties such as dolls, pottery, lacquer ware, silks, brocades, damascene, cloisonné and incense are concentrated here. Antique lovers should not miss two areas: **Shinmonzen St.**, just east of the Kamo River between Sanjo and Shijo Sts., and **Teramachi St.**, between Oike Dori and the Old Imperial Palace. These are probably the greatest concentrations of old things for sale in all Japan. A flea market is held at Toji Temple southwest of Kyoto Station on the 21st of each month. Textile fans can see how the city's *nishijin ori* and *yuzen* silks are made at centers explaining the processes. The **Nishijin Ori Kaikan** explains *nishijin* silk weaving as well as sells items made from the fabric.

Kodai Yuzen-en demonstrates how designs are hand painted on this type of silk. At **Nihon Shishukan** you can view and buy Japanese embroidery. If you enjoy the bustling activity of a morning food market, take an early-morning stroll through **Nishiki-no-Ichiba**, an alley which parallels Shijo Dori just to the north from Teramachi Dori to Horikawa Dori.

⑰ Tanakaya （田中彌　下京区四条通柳原馬場東入ル）

Right on Shijo Dori, this shop specializes in Kyoto dolls in their full splendor. Also has a display corner.

⑱ Oi Hyotan （大井ひょうたん　東山区清水3）

A six-foot-high gourd at the entrance tells what's inside — dried gourds in a wide array. Gourds were once used by the samurai to carry their sake on their belts — the sure sign of a playboy.

⑲ Erizen （ゑり善　下京区四条通河原町西）

Kimono maker to Kyoto's old families since 1584, and a gorgeous display, indeed. For about $2,000 you can order a nifty number in which you can slink around in your own bedroom.

⑳ Ishikawa Take-no-mise （石川竹の店　右京区嵯峨天竜寺造町35）

Out in Arashiyama, the Sagano district is thick with bamboo, and this shop has about 1,000 different things crafted with the wood — flower baskets, dolls, even holders for your tea cup. 9 a.m. to 6 p.m., closed Wed.

㉑ Tomatsuya （十松屋　上京区京都御所堺町御内の西）

One of the oldest fan dealers, turning out silver and gold works of art for the Imperial Household, classical Japanese dancers — or you. 9 a.m. to 8 p.m.

㉒ Jakko-in Kamado （寂光院窯　左京区大原寂光院前）

At the entrance to Jakko-in nunnery in Ohara, this shop lets you pick the clay object of your choice, paint it, then pick it up about 20 minutes later after baking. Cups, ash trays, pendants. 8:30 a.m. to 5:30 p.m.

San-nenzaka (near Kiyomizudera)

㉓ Tachikichi（たち吉 下京区四条小路）

On Shijo Dori, a famous pottery shop using old methods to make modern ceramics. The third floor has a nice selection of Kyoto's own *Kiyomizu-yaki* (*Kyo-yaki*).

㉔ Higashiyama Kogei（東山工芸 東山区高台寺北門入ル）

Near Yasaka Shrine, all of Kyoto's folk art specialties — masks, dolls, clay bells — are well stocked here.

㉕ Shogo-in Yatsuhashi（聖護院八ッ橋 聖護院山王町）

Kyoto's most famous pastry is a cinnamon and sugar-flavored rice cake known as *Yatsuhashi*, and this old shop created it back in 1689.

㉖ Inaba Shippo（稲葉七宝 東山区三条白川橋西入ル）

One of the most famous cloisonné shops in all Japan. Hand-painted enamelware on jewelry, cigarette cases, vases, etc.

㉗ Tanka（丹嘉 東山区本町22-504）

At Fushimi Inari Shrine, the small dolls of Kyoto people from the Edo era are actually amulets purchased by the shrine's pilgrims, but they make nice souvenirs.

㉘ Kyoto Handicraft Center（京都ハンディクラフトセンター 左京区丸太通東大路）

Built especially for foreign visitors, the tour buses never fail to bring you to this spot behind Heian Shrine. All the famous Kyoto products, but not necessarily for discriminating tastes. Let your eye be your guide.

NARA, UJI, OHARA & MT. HIEI

A 33-minute ride from Kyoto on the Kinki Nippon limited express train (¥670) brings you to **Nara**, Japan's first permanent capital and the door through which much Chinese influence came during its brief heyday from 710 to 784 A.D. The city's chief attractions are widely scattered, perhaps the most important being **Horyuji**, reached from Nara on the JNR Kansai Main Line (Horyuji Station-¥180). The worldly-wise Prince Shotoku who founded the temple in 607 A.D. made this place the fountainhead of Japanese art and culture. Its main hall may be the oldest surviving wooden structure in the world, and the treasure hall is filled with priceless objects from the period. The **Yumedono** (Hall of Dreams) is where the Prince meditated on Buddhist principles, and is noted for its octagonal shape. By taking the JNR Sakurai Line south from Nara to Sakurai (¥240), then the Kinki Nippon Railway about 10 minutes east to Hasedera (¥110) you'll reach **Hase Temple**, which climbs a steep hill through a forest of peony trees and is one of the most breathtakingly situated in all Japan. Nara lords used to flock out here for a rest, and you'll have no trouble understanding why. In Nara proper your first stop should be **Todaiji**, headquarters for the Kegon sect and all the temples in the provinces, and site of the country's biggest Buddha, almost 50-feet high. On the grounds are the **Shoso-in** (Treasure Depository), kept tightly sealed, except for a week in the fall when the rare works from the Nara period are put on view. The **Nara National Museum** near the entrance to **Nara Park** is open all year, however. Nearby, **Kofukuji Temple**'s five-story pagoda, especially when reflected in Sarusawa Pond, is practically a symbol of Nara. **Kasuga Shrine** is remarkable for some 3,000 stone lanterns which line its paths and are lit twice a year (February 3 or 4 and August 15). Call the Nara YMCA (0742)44-2207 for free student guide service a day in advance.

The Keihan Electric Railway will take you from Kyoto's Keihan-Sanjo Station to **Uji** in 40 minutes (¥200). **Byodo-in**, once the villa of Michinaga Fujiwara in the 10th century, became a monastery in 1052 and is today the finest example of architecture from the Fujiwara Period (794-1192 A.D.). Some architects have called its main hall the most beautiful building in the world. It houses a sculpture of the Amitabha Buddha in sublime repose. On your way back to Kyoto you might stop off at **Daigoji** to see Kyoto's oldest structure, a five-story pagoda, and the celebrated **Sambo-in**, the buildings and garden a great example of Hideyoshi's extravagant taste.

Two easy trips north of Kyoto are Ohara, a small village still retaining its country charm, and Mt. Hiei, site of the great Enryakuji Monastery and a Kyoto landmark. From Kyoto Station or Keihan-Sanjo Station it's a one hour bus ride to **Ohara** (¥340). You'll want to see **Sanzen-in**, noted for its lush garden full of pastels in the spring and rich reds

Kasuga Shrine (Nara)

and yellows in the fall. Some of the buildings were reconstructed from the ceremonial hall of the Old Imperial Palace. Across the valley is **Jakko-in**, a secluded nunnery founded by an Empress dowager who fled the world after her son's demise.

Mt. Hiei can be reached by bus from either Kyoto Station or Keihan-Sanjo Station in about one hour (¥560). The **Enryakuji Monastery** was founded in 788 A.D. at the top of this mountain by Saicho, founder of the Tendai sect, to protect Kyoto from the evil spirits which were suppose to come from the northeast. It later became a center of militant Buddhism, and its monks often swept down the mountain to stage raids, sometimes even threatening the Imperial Palace.

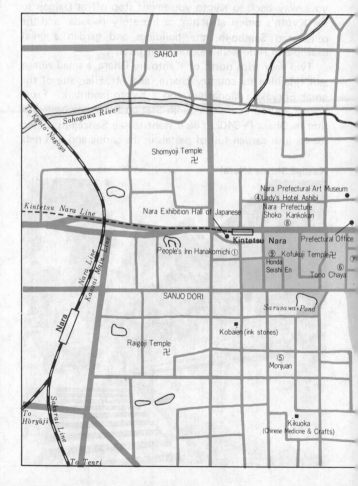

OHARA SLEEPING

Minshuku Ohara-Sanso, （民宿大原山荘）
17 Kusao-cho, Ohara, Sakyo-ku, (075)744-2227, 15 minutes from Ohara bus stop, beside Jakko-in. ¥4,400 with two meals.

Minshuku Ohara-no-sato, （民宿大原の里）
41 Kusao-cho, Sakyo-ku, (075)744-2917. A quiet retreat just outside Kyoto at entrance to Jakko-in. ¥4,400 with two meals.

Pension Yase Ohara （ペンション八瀬大原）
116-1 Yase Nose-Machi, Sakyo-ku, Ohara, (075) 722-6041. New pension convenient to Jakko-in and Sanzen-in. Just beside Yase Yuenchi bus stop. ¥4,400 per person without meals, ¥6,400 with dinner, breakfast.

NARA SLEEPING

❶ **People's Inn Hanakomichi** （ピープルズイン花小路）
23 Konishi-cho, (0742) 26-2646. Western-style. Near the Kintetsu Nara Station. Singles ¥4,400, twins ¥8,800.

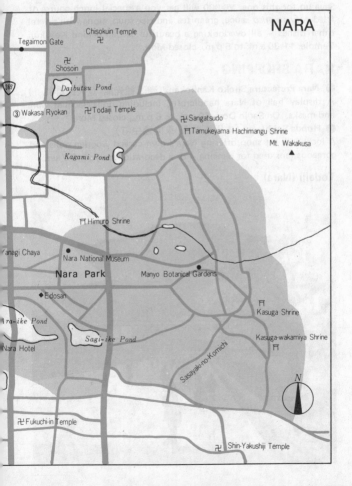

❷ Business Hotel Takatsuji　（ビジネスホテルたかつじ）
4-315 Shibatsuji-cho, (0742) 34-5371. A short walk from the Kintetsu Shin-Omiya Station. ¥4,400 per person without meals.

❸ Wakasa Ryokan　（わかさ旅館）
14 Oshiage-cho, (0742) 22-3143. ¥8,000 with two meals.

❹ Lady's Hotel Ashibi　（レディスホテル・馬酔木）
6-1 Kitamachi 1-chome, Higashimuki (0742) 26-7815. Ladies only. Japanese or western rooms at ¥4,000.

NARA EATS & DRINKS

❺ Monjuan　（文珠庵 勝南院町）
Tea or coffee amid old clocks, lamps and gramophones. 9 a.m. to 6 p.m.

❻ Tono Chaya　（塔の茶屋 登大路町47, Tel. (0742)22-4348）
A special *kayu bento* lunch for ¥2,000 is served on antique plates in this tea house. Antiques for sale. 11:30 a.m. to 9 p.m., closed Tues.

❼ Yanagi Chaya　（柳茶屋 登大路町4-48, Tel. (0742)22-7560）
Save up for this one. ¥6,000 will get you a special lunch course of fried *tofu* in *miso* sauce, green tea and rice soup, along with several other dishes — all overlooking a beautiful garden behind Kofukuji Temple. 11:30 a.m. to 6 p.m., closed Mon.

NARA SHOPPING

❽ Nara Prefecture Shoko Kankokan　（商工観光館 登大路町38-1）
A display hall of Nara handicrafts, including dolls, lacquer ware and masks. On Sanjo Dori. 10 a.m. to 6 p.m., closed Mon.

❾ Honda Seishi-en　（本田青紫園 東向通中町）
A local folk art shop offering Nara's own carved wooden dolls and gorgeous fans used for dancing — or a decoration on your TV set.

Todaiji (Nara)

HIMEJI

姫路

HIMEJI: IDYLLIC CASTLE

There's just one reason to get off the Bullet Train at Himeji about one hour west of Kyoto: the city has the finest extant Japanese castle in all the land.

During the bloody 16th century castles were built all over Japan, primarily as fortresses for protection against the enemy. Practically every *daimyo*, or regional lord, had one. Commonly there was a keep of several stories perched on either a natural or man-made hill supported by great, stone revetments laid in a graceful curve from bottom to top. The donjon was surrounded by outbuildings; tile-topped plaster walls and a series of moats to slow down an attacker's approach.

When things settled down in the 17th century under the Tokugawa *Shoguns,* the castles became less important as defense structures than as administrative headquarters for the region. Many a Japanese city grew up around a castle, with Tokyo the supreme example.

Himeji Castle (¥300, 9 a.m. to 4 p.m.) is not only still standing, but gorgeous, thanks to an eight-year repair job completed in 1964. Because of its stark, white walls topped by dark-gray tiles and the gentle curves of the roofs, the Japanese call it *Shirasagijo* or *Hakurojo* (egret castle). At a distance the structure does indeed look like a bird swooping over the rice fields.

If you can take your eyes off the donjon long enough, you'll discover a series of long structures and walkways spiraling up the hill. These separate buildings were the living quarters and dungeons, and this is the only castle where such buildings have survived. The buildings to the west of the donjon were built for Sen-hime, daughter of the second Tokugawa *Shogun* and wife to the son of the castle's *daimyo* in the early 17th century.

Himeji as we see it today was constructed between 1601—1610 by Terumasa Ikeda, son-in-law of Ieyasu Tokugawa, the first of the Tokugawa *Shoguns.* But the castle's origins can be traced to 1333 when a fortress was built here. That complex with the addition of a three-story donjon was used by Hideyoshi Toyotomi to conquer western Japan. It was from this castle that the great general launched an attack against the assassin of Nobunaga Oda. Nobunaga was murdered at Honnoji Temple in Kyoto in 1582.

HIMEJI SHOPPING

❶ **Kotobukiya** (ことぶきや　東二階町41)
This shop's wallets, gloves and handbags made of soft, white calve's leather are well known all over Japan.

❷ **Sanyo Department Store** (山陽デパート　直養町11-1)
Right in front of Himeji Station, with all the usual things, but the *hibashi* (fire tongs) here are an Himeji craft made by the Myochin family which got their start by making armor. The tongs are supposed to make a nice clinking sound. 10 a.m. to 6 p.m., closed Wed.

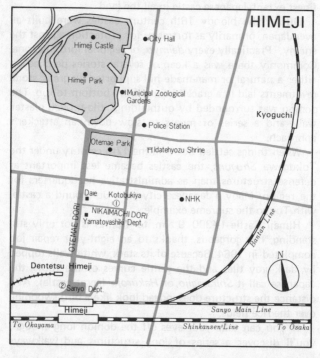

KURASHIKI

倉敷

KURASHIKI: GODOWN GALLERIES

If you like your art stylishly displayed, you'll like Kurashiki, where the town's old rice granaries distinctively covered half-way up their walls with black, clay tiles deeply set in white mortar, have been turned into art and archaeological museums and smart shops.

All of the city that matters for the visitor is a compact area on either side of a willow-lined canal about a 10-minute walk from Kurashiki Station. Away from the restored old buildings this is a growing industrial center making synthetic fiber, cotton yarn, petroleum, steel, machinery, chemicals and cement.

The chief attraction is the **Ohara Art Museum** (¥500, 9 a.m. to 5 p.m., closed Mon.) whose original building in neo-Greek style is impossible to miss amid the white walls and black tile roofs. The collection was put together by the late Mr. Ohara, president of what is now Kurabo Industries Ltd., and includes works by the best known French impressionists and El Greco's "Annunciation".

Within the grounds are also the **Ohara New Art Museum** with a small but interesting group of paintings by Japanese artists influenced by the impressionists (works by Shigeru Aoki, Ryuzaburo Umehara, Sotaro Yasui and Tsuguji Fujita are exceptional); the **Ohara Pottery Hall; Munakata Gallery; Serizawa Gallery** and **Far Eastern Gallery.**

The latter are in a group of old granaries as stunning for their interior design as for what's exhibited. The Pottery

Hall holds ceramics by the three great folk-style potters Shoji Hamada, Kanjiro Kawai and Kenkichi Tomimoto, plus some by the famous English Potter Bernard Leach. The Munakata and Serizawa Galleries are perhaps the best spots in all Japan to discover these famous artists, the former creating Buddhist-influenced woodblock prints and the latter stencil-dyed fabrics.

Steps from the Ohara compound are three other fine museums, each specializing in a different field. Although lodged in the usual Kurashiki godown, the interior of the **Kurashiki Art Museum** (¥300, 8:30 a.m. to 5 p.m.; June-Aug., 6 p.m.) would be quite at home in Paris or Vienna. The Ninagawa family collection of Western, Middle Eastern and ancient Mediterranean art includes ceramics, mosaics and sculpture.

Across the canal is the **Kurashiki Archaeological Museum** (¥300, 9 a.m. to 4:30 p.m., closed Mon.) with a small collection of Japanese artifacts, plus some pre-Columbian pottery and Peruvian textiles.

Further along the canal the **Kurashiki Folk Art Museum** (¥300, 9 a.m. to 5 p.m.; Dec.-Feb. 4:15 p.m., closed Mon.) has a wide assortment of Japanese folk art — rustic ceramics, glass, textiles, bamboo and wooden wares plus examples of rooms from Japanese homes—displayed in a group of connected warehouses.

You'll also want to wander a short distance from the canal to **Ivy Square**, a group of revitalized, 19th century, red-brick cotton mills, the first factory of Kurabo Industries. The complex now includes a hotel, restaurants and shops, and more small museums. The **Kurabo Memorial Hall** tells the history of the company. **The Kojima Gallery** displays western-style works by Okayama Prefecture native Torajiro Kojima who lived in Paris and helped Ohara purchase his French paintings. Ivy Square's courtyard paved with old bricks from the factory is a good spot to rest.

The standard covered shopping mall which is a feature in practically every Japanese city gets an extra plus here for the interesting craft shops at the Ohara Museum end. Look for *bizen-yaki*, a crude, deep-chestnut-colored pottery spotted with ash residue from wood-fired kilns; also woven reed products.

Thanks to the patronage of the town's native sons, Kurashiki has several good examples of modern Japanese architecture. The **Kurashiki International Hotel**, designed by Kurashiki-born Shizutaro Urabe who is now working in Osaka, features a three-story lobby filled with large murals by Munakata. The exterior, using the familiar black tiles set in white mortar, was designed to blend in with the nearby godowns. Urabe also designed Ivy

Square.

The peaceful canal with the swans was once busy with barges hauling rice from the warehouses to the Inland Sea, then to Osaka, the distribution center for all of Japan during the Tokugawa era. The surrounding fertile plain was and is a great rice producer.

For an overall look at the black tile roofs of the Old Town, climb the steps to **Kanryuji Temple**. Just 1 hour 20 minutes by bus from Kurashiki Station is **Washuzan Hill**, one of the best lookouts for a panorama of the island-dotted Inland Sea *(Seto Naikai)*.

The view may inspire you to linger, and a number of cruise ship and ferry services operate from the ports around it. STS *Ruto* (route) (Hiroshima (0822) 55-3344) operates a daily service from Onomichi (about one hour west of Kurashiki by JNR) to Setoda Island (departs 9:35 a.m., arrives Setoda 10 a.m. ¥1,780). From Setoda you can return to Onomichi (departs Setoda 3 p.m., arrives Onomichi 3:25 p.m.); or you can continue through the pine-clad islands on another STS ship to **Omijima**, noted for **Oyamazumi Shrine**, in fedual times a popular stopping point for soldiers off to battle, and containing some 80 percent of Japan's most valuable armor (not always on view); Hiroshima and Miyajima. Boats depart from Setoda for Miyajima at 1:45 p.m., stopping at Omijima at 2:05. There's an hour-and-a-half stop-over on Omijima to see the Shrine or admire the fine scenery. The boat departs again at 3:40, arriving in Hiroshima at 5 p.m., Miyajima at 5:20. (Setoda-Miyajima: ¥6,200). Taped explanations of the sights along the route are available in English. You can also start in Miyajima or Hiroshima and make the trip to Onomichi.

Except for the **Peace Memorial Museum** (¥50, 9 a.m.-4:30 p.m.) which chronicles the events of that fateful day August 6, 1945 when the city was virtually flattened by the world's first atomic bomb blast and makes a plea for world peace, there is no reason to tarry in Hiroshima proper. Lying in a river delta, it's never been in a naturally scenic spot, and little was done to rebuild the city in an attractive way after World War II.

The chief attraction in the Hiroshima area is **Miyajima** (Itsukushima) noted both for the beautiful scenery and **Itsukushima Shrine** whose great, red torii gates lie anchored in the water a short distance away from the attractive buildings connected by open corridors. Miyajima-guchi can be reached from Hiroshima by JNR in 25 minutes, then it's a 10-minute ferry ride across to the island; there is also boat service from Hiroshima.

KURASHIKI SLEEPING

❶ Kurashiki Station Hotel, (倉敷ステーションホテル)
Achi 2-chome, (0864)25-2525. Three minutes from the station, a short walk to the Ohara Museum. Singles ¥4,400, twins from ¥8,800.

❷ Kurashiki Tokusan Kan (倉敷特産館)
833 Hon-machi, (0864)25-3056. A conveniently located *minshuku* at the regular prices.

❸ Kurashiki International Hotel (倉敷国際ホテル)
1-14 Chuo-cho, 1-chome, (0864) 22-5141. Delightful, small western style hotel decorated with folk art. Just behind the Ohara Museum. Singles ¥7,600 up, twins ¥12,800 up.

❹ Kurashiki Terminal Hotel (倉敷ターミナルホテル)
7-2-901 Achi, 1-chome (0864) 26-1111. New. On top of an office building facing the station. Singles ¥4,290, twins ¥9,800.

❺ Ivy Hotel (アイビーホテル)
2 Hon-machi, 7-chome, (0864) 22-0011. Attractive rooms done up with local folk art, all tucked behind the red brick walls of the former Kurabo textile mill. Part of the Ivy Square complex. Singles ¥7,480, twins ¥11,360.

❻ Kurashiki (倉敷)
1 Hon-machi, 4-chome, (0864) 22-0730. A *minshuku* in old town near the museums. Standard rates.

❼ Tsurugata (つるがた)
3-15 Chuo-cho, 1-chome, (0864) 24-1635. Another *minshuku* right in old town and handy to all the sights. Standard rates.

KURASHIKI EATS & DRINKS

❽ El Greco (エル・グレコ 中央I-III, Tel. (0864)22-0297)
This landmark coffee shop has ivy-covered walls outside, high ceilings and warm woods with fresh flowers arranged in handsome Japanese ceramics inside. Right beside the Ohara Museum entrance. 10 a.m. to 5 p.m., closed Mon.

❾ Kohi Kan (珈琲館 本町4-I, Tel. (0864)24-5516)
Coffee with a view of the Old Town and served by an attractive mama-san. 10 a.m. to 5:30 p.m., closed Wed.

❿ Kamoi (カモ井 中央I-3-17, Tel. (0864)22-0606)
This *sushiya* (raw fish shop) specializes in fish slightly steamed in a bamboo container. There is an adjacent coffee shop. Right across from the Ohara Museum. 9a.m. to 7:30 p.m., closed Mon.

⓫ Onishi (おおにし 本町5-29, Tel. (0864)22-8134)
Home-made Japanese noodles from ¥500. Try their *zaru udon*, cold noodles which you dip in a spicy sauce, during the summer months. 10 a.m. to 6 p.m., closed Mon.

⓬ Tsuta
(蔦 本町7-2倉敷アイビースクエア内, Tel. (0864)22-0011)
Japanese style lunches from ¥800. But the specialty is a course of several fish and vegetable dishes served up in fine style at ¥3,500. 7:30-9:30 a.m.; 11:30 a.m. to 2 p.m.; 5 to 9 p.m.

KURASHIKI SHOPPING

⓭ Ivy Square (アイビースクエア 本町7-2)
The complex includes several shops. One sells a nice selection of Japanese folk art, including reed crafts and *washi* paper. 8 a.m. to 7 p.m.

⓮ Nihon Kyodo Gangukan (日本郷土玩具館 中央1-4-16)
Toys from everywhere for from ¥200. 8 a.m. to 5 p.m.

⓯ Kura (倉 本町5-25)
A godown full of crafts just beside the canal. 9 a.m. to 5:30 p.m., closed Mon.

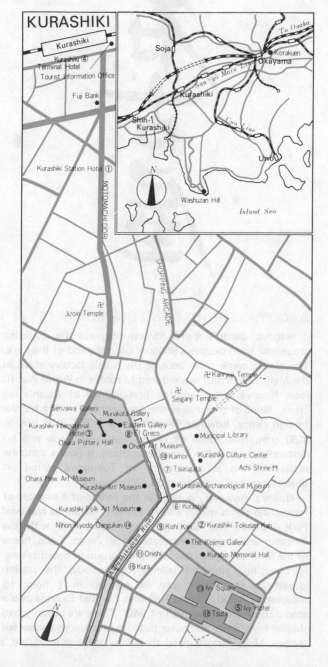

NAGOYA

NAGOYA: SHRINES AND CORMORANTS

Nagoya, Japan's fourth largest city, was the stomping ground of the Tokugawa Shoguns until the end of their era. The classic castle town became the classic factory town in the Meiji period and was reduced to rubble in World War II. Now Nagoya is perhaps the best-planned of Japan's big cities. None of this makes the city very interesting for the foreign visitor, however. **Nagoya Castle** (¥250, 9:30 a.m. to 4:30 p.m.) the home of Ieyasu Tokugawa's son and his descendants until the Meiji Restoration, is now a concrete replica serving as a museum for Tokugawa period art objects, especially paintings on sliding doors.

Nagoya, however, is right in the center of a number of interesting sights within a day's journey. **Ise-Shima National Park** includes **Ise Shrine**, closely associated with the Emperor and the most venerated in all Japan; Toba, home of the Mikimoto pearl domain; and a group of breathtakingly beautiful, pine-clad islands. Uji-Yamada, the station closest to the shrine, can be reached in 1 hour 18 minutes by Kinki Nippon Railways Limited Express over a scenic route from Nagoya (¥1,640). There are actually two shrines here, inner and outer outdoor sanctuaries connected by bus. Most visitors spend their time at the inner shrine, a

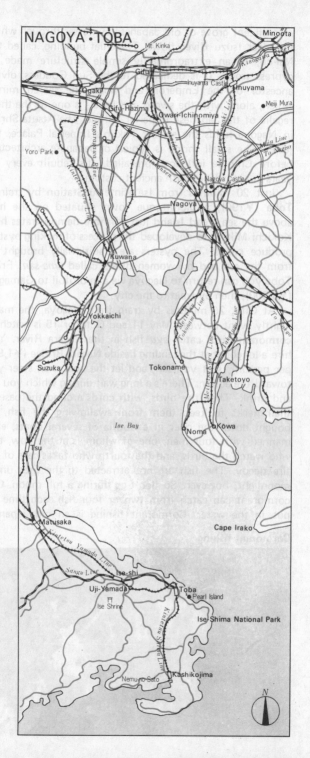

magnificent grove of old Japanese cypresses through which the clear Isuzu River flows. The chief building, called the Nai-ku, is an extraordinarily simple structure made of cypress wood. It is dedicated to the Sun Goddess, divine ancestor of the Emperor, and holds the sacred mirror which, along with the sword and jewel, is one of the three regalia of the Japanese Imperial Throne. The Atsuta Shrine in Nagoya holds the sword; Tokyo's Imperial Palace, the jewel. The small shrine is typical of Japanese architecture before Chinese influence prevailed. It's rebuilt every 20 years in accordance with ancient custom.

Just 20 minutes from Ise Kintetsu Station by train is **Toba** (¥190), a picturesque town situated on the hills above the sea. **Pearl Island** just offshore demonstrates how Kokichi Mikimoto developed the process of making oysters produce pearls. The oysters are traditionally brought up from the sea bed by women divers called *ama-san*. From Toba you can return to Nagoya via a hydrofoil to Gamagori (¥3,300), then by train to the city.

At Gifu, 26 minutes by train from Nagoya, the major nightly event between May 11 and October 15 is watching **cormorant birds** catch *ayu* fish in the Nagara River. You hire a longboat at the landing beside Nagara Bridge (¥1,900 per person), seat yourself, and let the boatsmen steer you toward the action. There's a long wait during which you eat and drink. Then the birds, with cords around the base of their necks to keep them from swallowing the fish, are bought down the river in a flotilla of several boats, each manned with four men, one of whom is at the bow, two who watch the birds, and the fourth who takes care of the fire decoy. The fish are not attracted to the fires under moonlight, however. So don't go during a full moon. One cormorant can catch from two or four fish each time it's put in the water. Cormorant fishing is an old Japanese

Cormorant fishing

custom which can also be seen at Arashiyama and Uji near Kyoto and Hakata on Kyushu.

The sport is also done on the Kiso River at nearby **Inuyama**, a city famous for its small, white castle dating from 1440, the oldest in the country, from which there is a fine view of the river's rapids. The Kiso is known as Japan's Rhine between Inuyama and the villages of Rhine-Yuen and Imawatari upstream. **Imawatari** is a 55-minute train ride on the Meitetsu Line from Shin-Nagoya Station (¥490). There are public and private boats for hire (¥2,400), and you can shoot the rapids to Inuyama in about two hours.

Southeast of Inuyama is **Meiji Mura** (Meiji Village) (¥1,000, 10 a.m. to 5 p.m.), an outdoor Museum of buildings from the Meiji period, Japan's Victorian age. There are 39 structures in all, and especially interesting is a small-town *kabuki* theater and the original facade from Tokyo's famous Imperial Hotel designed by American architect Frank Lloyd Wright — not a Meiji era building, but here, nevertheless. Meiji Mura can also be reached by Meitetsu Express Bus direct from its Nagoya bus terminal to the gate (¥860). The trip takes 60 minutes.

An hour and a half from Nagoya on the JNR Chuo Main Line will bring you to Nagiso from where it's a short bus or taxi ride to **Tsumago**, one of Japan's best preserved old towns nestled in a mountain valley on the old stone-paved Nakasendo Road which was used as an alternate route between Edo (Tokyo) and Kyoto during the Tokugawa era. The town shares the limelight with **Magome**, another old village a 20-minute bus ride or a two or three-hour hike away, for being unspoiled; but Tsumago gives a better sense of the past in a mountain road stage stop: a single street of old wooden shops and homes. There are many *minshuku*. At Kameyama ((02645) 7-3187)), a 20-minute walk above Tsumago, the owner serves up her

Meiji Mura   **Kiso Rapids**

own fresh trout, mountain greens and pickles (¥4,000 with two meals) as a sample.

NAGOYA SLEEPING

Nagoya Crown Hotel (名古屋クラウンホテル)
Sakae 1-chome, Naka-ku, (052) 211-6633. Five minutes from the Fushimi subway station. Singles from ¥4,000, twins from ¥6,600.

Hotel Sun Route Nagoya (ホテルサンルート名古屋)
Sakae 1-chome, Naka-ku (052) 221-7011. A 10-minute walk from Nagoya Station. Singles from ¥3,300, twins from ¥8,900.

Dai-ichi Washington Hotel (第一ワシントンホテル)
Nishiki 3-chome, Naka-ku, (052) 951-2111. Just a minute from the Sakae subway station. Singles from ¥3,400, twins from ¥7,200.

Nagoya Chisan Hotel (名古屋チサンホテル)
Noritake 1-chome, Nakamura-ku, (052) 452-3211. A few minutes walk from Nagoya Station. Singles ¥4,100, twins ¥7,800.

Parkside Hotel (パークサイドホテル)
6-15 Nishiki, 3-chome, Naka-ku, (052) 971-1131. Handy location near Sakae subway station. Situated right in front of TV tower. Singles from ¥4,900, twins from ¥7,500.

Ekimae Monblanc Hotel (駅前モンブランホテル)
14-1 Meiki, 3-chome, Nakamura-ku, (052) 541-1121. Right beside the JNR Nagoya Station. Singles from ¥4,960, twins from ¥8,250.

Tokyu Inn (東急イン)
17-18 Marunouchi, 2-chome, Naka-ku, (052) 202-0109. Three minutes from the JNR Nagoya Station. Singles from ¥6,300, twins from ¥9,200.

Nagoya Plaza Hotel (ナゴヤプラザホテル)
8-21 Nishiki, 3-chome, Naka-ku, (052) 951-6311. Brand new, just beside the Sakae subway station. Singles from ¥3,960, twins from ¥6,930.

Nagoya Castle

TAKAYAMA

TAKAYAMA: LIFE IN THE MOUNTAINS

Four fifths of the Japanese archipelago is covered by mountains — some gentle like those around Kyoto, some wild and rugged like the Japan Alps. Probably no single topographical feature of the land has had a greater impact on the Japanese mind.

For practically all Japanese, home was or is a valley. Many villages are built beside a swiftly running stream. Every patch of level land beside the water is planted with something, principally rice, and in some areas the paddies are built on terraces right up the mountainsides.

Where the valleys were especially broad, the major cities grew. Tokyo, Osaka, Nagoya — each was built on a marshy plain through which sweep several rivers.

Takayama is special because, perhaps more than any other town in the mountains, it's been able to preserve its old houses and shops and godowns — not a single, isolated, wooden house overpowered by a concrete monstrosity next door, but whole blocks full of wooden slat facades and deep, overhanging roofs. Many of the houses are open to the public, providing a great opportunity for the visitor to learn what life was like where winters were long and hard and at no time was life exactly easy.

Right in front of the exit from Takayama Station the city has a **Tourist Information Office** which can give you an English map of the town and make a *minshuku* reservation. Also in front of the station you can rent a bicycle for from

¥200 for one hour to ¥1,000 for the day. Since the city is small and relatively traffic-free, it's a pleasant place to cycle.

The old and most interesting parts of town for the tourist lie east of the station between the Miya and Enako Rivers and between the Hachiman Shrine on the north and Shiroyama Park, site of the former local castle, to the south.

A good place to start is the **Takayama Jinya** (¥200, 8:45 a.m. to 5 p.m.; Nov.-Mar., 4:30 p.m., closed Wed.) on the west bank of the Miya River below Shiroyama. This was one of 60 regional administrative offices established by the Tokugawa Shogun in the late 17th century, and the only

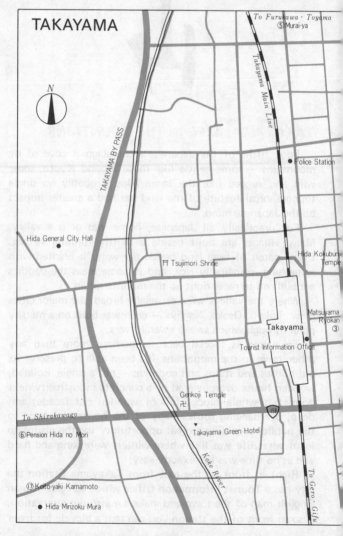

one remaining. After passing through an impressive gate, you can stroll through the *tatami* rooms of the offices, a rice repository and storehouses.

Across Nakabashi Bridge, painted bright red, and to the left is a block full of well preserved, **old merchants' shops,** many of them turned into gift stores selling local souvenirs. Continue on the same street across the next intersection, and the 19th century Japan mood continues, although a few modern intrusions have crept in.

There are several combination shops and homes of rich merchants open, each characterized by a spacious, two-story high foyer with open-beam ceilings. An interesting feature is the *irori*, or open hearth sunk into the tatami

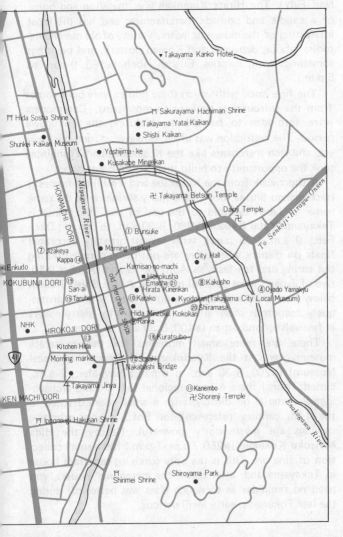

floor, around which the customers huddled during the frosty winters. A screen was often placed behind the guests' backs to ward off the draft. The family lived in smaller rooms behind the sliding doors and opening out into small gardens.

Perhaps the most impressive of the three merchants' homes open to the public is the **Kusakabe Mingeikan** (Kusakabe Folklore Museum) which, despite the name, is more interesting for the building than the folk art it contains (¥200, 9 a.m. to 5 p.m.; Dec.-Feb., 4:30 p.m., closed Fri.). If you want to see more of this interesting architecture, also drop by the **Yoshijima-ke**, next door neighbor to Kusakabe (¥200, 9 a.m. to 5 p.m.; closed Tues., Nov.-Feb.). The **Hirata Kinenkan** was the shop and home of a candle and pomade manufacturer and has the most interesting of the museums, with a variety of old merchants' tools, fabrics, Japanese and Korean pottery, and paintings sometimes with, surprise, English labels (¥180, 9 a.m. to 5 p.m.).

The fine wood with which these homes were built comes from the surrounding timber-rich mountains. Commoners were forbidden to cut the trees during the Tokugawa period. The restriction was lifted, however, during the Meiji era, and rich merchants like the Kusakabes and Yoshijimas took the opportunity to build their dream house/shop.

A short walk from the Kusakabe and Yoshijima homes is **Hachimangu Shrine**, one of the many shrines with the same name in Japan devoted to the god of war. Next door is **Takayama Yatai Kaikan** (¥380, 8:30 a.m. to 5 p.m.; Dec.-Feb., 9 a.m.-4:30 p.m.), with several ornately decorated floats on display when they are not being paraded during the spring and fall festivals April 14-15 and October 9-10, two of Japan's most colorful pageants. At the **Shishi Kaikan** below Hachiman is a new museum devoted to those grotesquely humorous *shishi* (lion) masks worn by merrymakers at festivals around Japan (¥400, 8:30 a.m. to 5 p.m.).

There are more small museums for the inveterate museum-goer. At the **Kyodokan** (Takayama City Local Museum) (¥200, 8:30 a.m. to 5 p.m.; Nov.-Mar., 9 a.m., closed Thurs.) there is more regional folk art and archaeological material on display, with a small room devoted to the 17th century priest-sculptor Enkū, whose primitive carvings are mysteriously powerful. Nearby the **Hida Minzoku Kokokan** (¥250, 7 a.m.-7 p.m.) has a small collection of fine art. This is the only surviving samurai's house in Takayama and, after seeing the merchants' houses, you need no reminder as to which class was better off during the late Tokugawa, early Meiji periods.

The **Hida Kokubunji** with a fine, three-story pagoda, is the oldest temple in the city. Founded in 1588, it was one of the provincial temples put under the direction of Todaiji Temple you met back in Nara. An enormous gingko tree, pure gold in autumn, dominates the small grounds.

A bicycle will be handy to reach the **Hida Minzoku Mura** (¥300, 8:30 a.m. to 5 p.m.; Nov.-Mar., 4:30 p.m.) a village of country houses about one mile from the station. This is the most accessible place in all of Japan to grasp the conditions in which the vast majority of the mountain common people — chiefly the farmers and craftsmen in the Tokugawa period — eked out their frugal lives.

The high-pitched, thatched-roofs, called *gassho-zukuri* (in the shape of hands in prayer) kept the snow from piling high. In the multi-storied versions of these homes the upper floors, dark and dry from the smoke of the *irori* on the main floor, were used to rear silkworms, an occupation that kept several families busy during the summer months. As many as 50 or 60 people sometimes lived in the structures. Another house features strong beams supporting a shingle roof over which stones were laid to keep the wind from ripping it off. Homes of a village headman and a Buddhist priest, and a rice storehouse are also displayed. From the site there is a fine view of the usually snow-capped Alps.

On a mountaintop just east of the city (a 15-minute bus ride to Shūkokan-mae, then about a one hour hike uphill) is **Senkōji**, an old temple neglected over the years, but once a stopping-off-place for the much-traveled priest-sculptor Enkū, whose works you saw at the Kyodokan in town. More of his sculpture is on view at the adjacent **Enkū Exhibition Hall** (¥300, 9 a.m. to 5 p.m.).

If you want to see thatched-roof houses still occupied, you'll have to venture to **Shirakawago Gassho Mura** (¥300) where eight of these homes were transported from a dam site and are open from 8:30 a.m. to 5 p.m. It's a

Old Merchant Houses

1-hour 35-minute bus ride from Takayama to Makido (¥1,400), then another 1 hour by JNR bus (¥980) to Ogimachi, site of the village and several *minshuku*.

A scenic 1-hour bus ride (¥1,050) to **Hirayu Onsen** will bring you to one of the country's less-spoiled mountain spas. About 20 *ryokan* (Japanese inns) and *minshuku* are clustered here at the foot of Mt. Norikura, and some of them feature outdoor baths from which you can gaze at the midnight stars.

When a Japanese takes a holiday, it's often at an *onsen*. The volcanic island chain has thousands of natural springs emitting waters believed to be good for one ailment or another. Feeling better is part of the lure. But the *onsen* conjures romantic images — relaxing in a hot pool with a view of nature's wonders, strolling around the area in your cotton kimono and, for the men, perhaps a flirtation or two with an *onsen* geisha a la Yasunari Kawabata's "Snow Country" novel.

Today, however, any *onsen* that can be reached by bus — and that includes most of them — will probably disappoint you. The old, wooden inns have mostly been replaced with high-rise *hoteru*, armies of drunk and over-happy octogenarians, business-minded bar hostesses and striptease parlors. The scenery, thank God, is still there. Before you eagerly head for an *onsen*, try to find out what the place is like.

Jinya (Takayama)

TAKAYAMA SLEEPING

There are many *minshuku*. The following are only a few suggestions. You can get help from the city tourist office at the station exit for accommodations either in Takayama or up in the mountains at Hirayu Onsen.

❶ Bunsuke, （文助）
77 Shimoichino-cho, (0577)33-0315.

❷ Iiyama-so, （いいやま荘）
262-2 Honobu-cho, (0577)33-4863.

❸ Matsuyama Ryokan （まつやま旅館）
5-11 Hanazato-cho, (0577)32-1608.

❹ Oyado Yamakyu （お宿山久）
58 Tenshoji (0577)32-3756. 15 minutes by foot from the JNR station.

❺ Murai-ya （村井屋）
148 Honobu-cho (0577)33-4823.

❻ Pension Hida no Mori （ペンションひだの杜）
3349 Shingu-cho (0577)34-6575. Western-style rooms.

TAKAYAMA EATS & DRINKS

In this mountain area the specialties are mountain greens *(sansai)*, lake trout *(masu)* and various types of mushrooms and nuts. Be sure and try the *mitarashi dango*, small rice cakes roasted on a stick over a charcoal fire.

❼ Jizakeya （地酒屋 末広町 2 番街, Tel. (0577)34-5001）
Japanese snacks such as grilled meat *(yakiniku)* and bean curd *(tofu)* – and 13 kinds of local sake. ¥2,500-¥3,500. 4 p.m.- 2 a.m.

❽ Kakusho （角正 馬場2-98, Tel. (0577)32-0174）
Their ¥6,000 and ¥6,500 vegetarian lunch of mountain vegetables, noodles, mushroom soup and sugared nuts is not exactly in the bargain category, but save up for this special treat. The food is served in a tea house overlooking a garden. Lunch only, 11:30 a.m.- 1:30 p.m., closed Thurs. Reservations required.

Hida Sake

Mitarashi Dango Stand

❾ Ranka（藍花 上三之町93, Tel. (0577)32-3887）
Coffee (¥300) and good ice cream (¥450) in a mud-walled, old warehouse.

❿ Karako（唐子 上三之町90, Tel. (0577)32-0244）
Japanese green powder tea *(maccha)* and sweet-bean cakes sold in sets from ¥350; also *amazake*, a sweet, thick sake served warm (¥350), in a rustic Hida setting.

⓫ Kanembo（嘉念坊 堀端町8, Tel. (0577)33-0776）
More vegetarian food served in Shorenji Temple. ¥4,000, ¥5,000 and ¥6,000 courses. 11 a.m.-6 p.m. Reservations required.

⓬ Susaki（洲さ起 神明町4-14, Tel. (0577)32-0023）
Sansai — greens fresh from the nearby mountains — is the specialty of this quality establishment. ¥8,000 course. 11:30 a.m.-7 p.m. Reservations required.

⓭ Kitchen Hida（キッチン飛騨 本町1-66, Tel. (0577)32-5406）
Beef from the area mountain grazing lands served in courses in the ¥5,000-¥7,000 price range.

⓮ Kappa（かっぱ 朝日町, Tel. (0577)33-8909）
Izakaya drinking place with *kushiyaki* (meat and vegetables grilled on bamboo sticks) and *sansai* as the specialities.

⓯ Taruhei（樽平 有楽町3, Tel. (0577)32-5490）
A *nomiya* drinking place which draws the locals for sake fresh from the keg.

TAKAYAMA SHOPPING

Several types of pottery are produced in Takayama, the most striking of which is *shibukusa-jiki*, a fine, white porcelain with hand-painted, deep-blue designs. The **Hōkokusha** shop selling this ceramic is across the intersection and a few doors to the right on the same street where the Hirata Kinenkan is located. The town is also famous for its *shunkei-nuri*, a clear lacquer ware which allows the wood's natural grains to show through. You can see the full array of the latter at the **Shunkei Kaikan Museum**. In a region full of fine timber, wood carvings are naturally common. Antique shops loaded with odds and ends from the last century are scattered throughout the old neighborhoods. Don't miss the **morning markets**

either in front of Takayama Jinya or along the Miya River. Country people from the surrounding mountains are here from 7 a.m. till noon with fresh vegetables, fruit and crafts.

⑯ Enkudo （円空洞　天満町6飛騨国分寺境内）

Just inside the main gate of Kokubunji Temple, this tiny old farm house is the working place of master wood carver Toshiro Miwa who creates surprising likenesses of the Buddha carved by Enkū that you saw at the Kyodokan. Also miniatures of Takayama's festival floats, folk toys and dolls made of Japanese paper. 8 a.m. to 9 p.m.

⑰ Koito-yaki Kamamoto （小糸焼窯元　上岡本町1037）

Located at Hida Minzoku Mura, potter Mitsuro Hasekura's rustic works are for sale here — all with a country flavor.

⑱ Kuratsubo （倉坪　上一之町8）

A 30-year-old antique shop offering pottery, chests and old house wares from the region, not necessarily at a poor man's prices. Browse anyway. 8:30 a.m. to 5:30 p.m.

⑲ San-ai （山愛　相生町23）

Easy to spot with a water wheel outside, this shop has all the local goodies — folk art, including pottery, straw hats, Hida pickles and bean paste.

⑳ Shiramasa （志良政　馬場町1）

Rustic antiques from the not-too-distant past.

㉑ Emacha （江間茶　上之一色町）

A curio shop offering possibilities for your living room shelf.

Irori

KANAZAWA

KANAZAWA: CLASSY CASTLE TOWN

Of the many Japanese cities built around a castle, Kanazawa stands out. It was dominated during the Tokugawa era by the Maeda *daimyos*, the richest in all the land, by virtue of the amount of rice grown in their territory. Such stature brought culture. It also created what is common to potentates everywhere: paranoia. To the Tokugawa *Shogun* the Maedas were outside lords not wholly trusted. So they quite naturally did everything possible to prevent the *Shogun* from exercising any wrath.

The Maeda castle was protected not only by the usual high walls and moats. It was also surrounded by winding, twisting streets. The two rivers on either side acted as further barriers. And for more good measure, the temples of the Buddhist sects favored by the Tokugawas were placed at the approach from Edo on the other side of the Saigawa River. One of these was not really a temple at all, but an escape hatch connected by tunnel to the castle. Tokugawa spies were everywhere in the land passing on to Edo any information hinting of insurrection.

With a population as eager as any in Japan to be "modern", Kanazawa is not totally a city of the past. But thanks to having been spared the bombings of World War II, there is enough left to give a quite clear picture of life in a Japanese castle town. All you need is a little imagination to replace what's now a modern building.

Start at Kanazawa's reason for being, the castle, now the

site of Kanazawa University. Unfortunately, all that's left of it is **Ishikawa Gate**, merely the back door during its heyday. The cautious Maedas were ever-ready for the worst. Those lovely white tiles on the roof could be melted down for ammunition, if necessary.

Kanazawa's great sightseeing attraction is **Kenrokuen** across the street from Ishikawa Gate. This garden is considered, along with Okayama's Korakuen and Mito's Kairakuen, as one of Japan's "three greatest" stroll gardens. Landscaping began as early as 1670 under the fifth Maeda *daimyo*, but it wasn't completed in its present form until the early 19th century under the 13th Maeda lord.

The Japanese have given a name to practically every tree, rock and blade of grass here. The tourists swarm through in groups, their leaders giving the details through a loudspeaker as they rush by. The gates open at 6:30 a.m.. April-October, however, and if you're an early bird, you can avoid the pandemonium.

Seisonkaku Villa (¥400, 8:30 a.m. to 4:30 p.m., closed Wed.), a sumptuous, Japanese-style home built by the 13th lord for his retiring mother, stands inside the garden and is well worth a few minutes' peek to see how comfortable a retired grandmother can be.

Just outside the garden and behind Seisonkaku is the **Ishikawa Prefectural Art Museum** (¥200, 9 a.m. to 4 p.m.) with a permanent collection of Kutani ceramics, one of the city's most famous products. Kutani ware has had its ups and downs: Its makers were patronized by the Maeda family from around the mid-1600s, but for reasons unknown, production stopped entirely, then was revived about 100 years later. The old Kutani (Ko-Kutani) is highly prized and extraordinary for its rich color combinations of corn yellow, deep green and lavender. Today Kutani ware is produced in an amazing variety and every tourist shop has it. Ko-Kutani, however, can these days be found only in the most expensive antique shops. If it suits your taste, some of the modern potters copy the colors and patterns of the old ceramics closely.

Before wandering away from Kenrokuen a stop at **Gyokusenen Garden** (¥300, 9 a.m. to 4 p.m., closed Dec.-Mar.) another stroll garden, but on a far more manageable scale, is a special treat. Unless you're royalty, you'll feel a lot more comfortable ambling over the stepping stones and through the moss and maple trees here than at the *daimyo*'s version of the same above.

There are several small museums within a short walk of Kenrokuen which will help round out the picture of how the lord's retainers lived. Just down the hill from the Ishikawa Prefectural Museum is the **Honda Museum** (¥400,

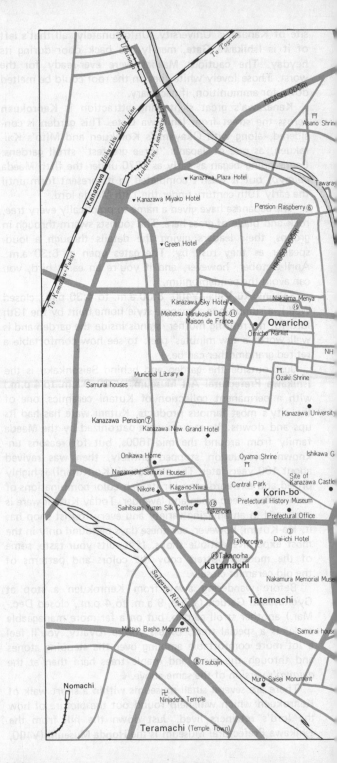

To Toyama

To Uchinada

Higashi Odori

Hokuriku Main Line

Hokutetsu Asanogawa Line

Kanazawa

Asano Shrine

Kanazawa Plaza Hotel

Tawaray

Kanazawa Miyako Hotel

Pension Raspberry ⑥

Hikoso Odori

Green Hotel

To Komatsu · Fukui

Kanazawa Sky Hotel ▾

Nakajima Menya ⑲

Meitetsu Marukoshi Dept ⑪
Maison de France

Owaricho

Ōmicho Market

NH

Municipal Library ●

Ozaki Shrine

Samurai houses

Kanazawa University

Kanazawa Pension ⑦

Kanazawa New Grand Hotel

Onikawa Home

Oyama Shrine

Ishikawa G

Nagamachi Samurai Houses

Nikore

Kaga-no-Niwa

Central Park

Site of
Kanazawa Castle

Korin-bo

Saihitsuan Yuzen Silk Center

⑫

Takenban

Prefectural History Museum

Prefectural Office

③

Dai-ichi Hotel

⑭ Moroeya

⑬ Taka-no-ha

Katamachi

Nakamura Memorial Muse

Tatemachi

Saigawa River

Matsuo Basho Monument

Samurai house

⑧ Tsubajin

Nomachi

Muro Saisei Monument

卍
Ninjadera Temple

Teramachi (Temple Town)

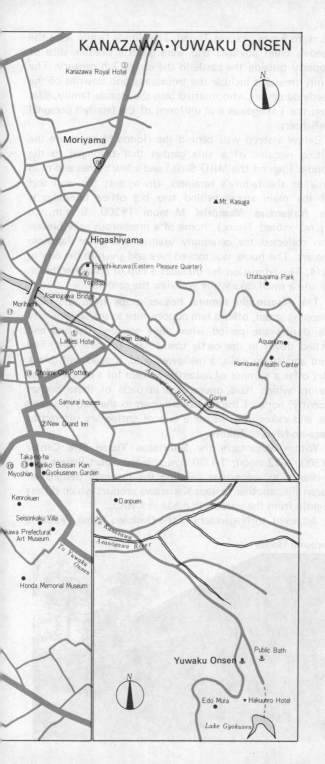

KANAZAWA・YUWAKU ONSEN

Kanazawa Royal Hotel ①

Moriyama

▲ Mt. Kasuga

Higashiyama

■ Higashi-kuruwa (Eastern Pleasure Quarter)
④ Yogetsu

Asanogawa Bridge

Utatsuyama Park

Morihachi ⑰

⑤ Ladies Hotel

Tenjin Bashi

Aquarium ●
● Kanazawa Health Center

⑯ Choami Ohi Pottery

Samurai houses

Goriya ⑨

②New Grand Inn

Taka-no-ha
⑩ ⑬● Kanko Bussan Kan
Miyoshian ● Gyokusen Garden

Kenrokuen ●

Seisonkaku Villa ●

Ikawa Prefectural
Art Museum ●

Honda Memorial Museum ●

● Danpuen

To Kanazawa

Asanogawa River

To Yuwaku Onsen

Public Bath
Yuwaku Onsen ♨ ♨

Edo Mura ● ▼ Hakuunro Hotel

Lake Gyokusen

115

9 a.m. to 5 p.m., except Thurs). The Honda family were the Maeda's chief advisors and were given a sizeable slice of property outside the castle in the early 17th century. The family treasures include the trousseaux and dowries of the Maeda daughters who married into the Honda family, gifts from the Tokugawas and uniforms of the family's personal firefighters.

Below a steep wall behind the Honda Museum are the wilting remains of a villa garden that belonged to the Hondas (behind the MRO Bldg.) and a few homes and mud walls of the family's retainers. Up against the wall and off the main street behind two big office buildings is the **Nakamura Memorial Museum** (¥200, 9 a.m. to 4 p.m., closed Thurs.), home of a prosperous sake brewer who collected tea ceremony utensils and other Japanese fine art. The house was moved here and given to the city in 1974. The admission fee includes a cup of powdered green tea and a small cake while you view the garden.

The **Nagamachi samurai houses**, steps from the main shopping street, offer a rare opportunity to see samurai city life during the period when they stopped fighting and settled down in the castle towns next to their lord. The mud and straw walls, a mellowed gold, topped with black tiles offer a glimpse of austerity. Except for a couple of tea parlors which have opened up in parts of these houses recently, none of the homes are open to the public. Green tea and cakes in a set, or a cup of coffee are offered at **Kaga-no-Niwa** or **Nikore.**

Within Nagamachi the **Saihitsuan Yuzen Silk Center** (¥300, 9-12 noon; 1-4:30 p.m., closed Thurs.) gives you a chance to see artists painting the intricate designs on *yuzen* silk, another famous Kanazawa product which differs slightly from the *yuzen* silk made in Kyoto.

Adjacent to Nagamachi is the **Onikawa home** (¥300, 8

Samurai House

a.m. to 6 p.m. (9-5 in winter)), a fine, 200-year-old house brought here and placed on what was once the exclusive property of a samurai by a wealthy industrialist from Daishoji town. The house is built around a lovely small garden with a winding stream which can also be viewed from the coffee shop next door.

On the other side of the Saigawa River and a 10-minute walk from the main shopping street lies **Teramachi** (temple town), the spot where the Maeda *daimyo* placed temples favored by the Tokugawas as an additional defense measure. Most of these temples are run-down and of little interest except for the silence they offer, but one is the biggest tourist attraction next to Kenrokuen. Called Myōritsuji (¥300), it's more popularly known as **Ninjadera** (spy temple) after the Tokugawa spies who rampantly sniffed out any malcontent. The innocent looking temple is loaded with secret chambers, trap doors, hidden staircases — all built around a well which was a tunnel to the Saigawa River and the castle. Reservations are necessary (0762) 41-2877.

Save time for **strolling along the quays** on either of the two rivers, the stretch between the Asano River Bridge and Tenjin Bashi beside the Asano River being especially nice. Another breathing space is **Central Park** just beside the shopping area. Park yourself on a bench, and within minutes you'll be attracting students from nearby Kanazawa University who want to see if they can understand your English.

Outside Kanazawa, it's well worth the ¥450, 45-minute bus ride to **Yuwaku Onsen**, a tiny hot-spring resort distinguished for the fanciful, luxurious **Hakuunro Hotel**, a Spanish-Chinese architectural marvel hanging off a verdant cliff, and Edo Mura, a group of buildings from the Edo period. The bus stops in front of the hotel. A short walk up the road will bring you to the **Edo Mura** entrance (¥700, 8

Kenrokuen in Winter

a.m. to 6 p.m., 5 p.m. Nov.-Mar.). Among the structures brought here are a country inn where the Emperor Meiji once stayed and several farmers', merchants' and samurais' homes. The Hakuunro is too expensive for the bargain traveler, but have a snack in the coffee shop before you head back to town. In Yuwaku village below you can try the public bath (1-10 p.m.) for a few hundred yen.

Kanazawa is one of the few cities outside the Tokyo-Kyoto orbit about which there is a thorough guidebook in English. If you're thinking about spending any time here, be sure and pick up a copy of **"Kanazawa: The Other Side of Japan"** (see Bibliography). The City of Kanazawa also publishes an excellent English-language map including tourist information, available at the city tourist information office in front of Kanazawa Station or at the Kanko Bussankan beside Kenrokuen.

KANAZAWA SLEEPING

❶ **Kanazawa Royal Hotel**（金沢ロイヤルホテル）
Kogane-machi 3-chome, (0762)52-7151. Five minutes from Kanazawa Station. Singles from ¥4,000, twins from ¥7,700.
❷ **New Grand Inn,**（ニューグランドイン）
Kenroku Moto-machi, (0762)22-1211. Convenient and quiet location, steps from Kenrokuen, with a good coffee shop serving a ¥700 western breakfast. Singles ¥5,300, twins ¥10,500.
❸ **Kanazawa Dai-ichi Hotel**（金沢第一ホテル）
Hirosaka Dori, (0762)22-2011. Also right beside Kenrokuen. Singles ¥4,000, twins ¥7,200.
❹ **Yogetsu,**（陽月）
1-13-22 Higashiyama, (0762)52-0497. A *minshuku* in an old geisha house in the city's classiest geisha quarter. ¥4,500.
❺ **Kanazawa Ladies Hotel,**（金沢レディスホテル）
10-38 Hashiba-cho, (0762)22-1531. Ladies only in a pretty location right beside the Asano River. ¥4,000.
❻ **Pension Raspberry,**（ペンションラズベリー）
25-27 Hyotan-machi, (0762)23-0757. Convenient to Musashi section, run by a charming couple who have traveled all over Europe. ¥4,000, including breakfast. Beds, not *futon*.
❼ **Kanazawa Pension**（金沢ペンション）
8-4 Nagamachi, 3-chome, (0762)61-3489. A cozy *minshuku* in the Nagamachi samurai house quarter and a 10-minute walk to Kenrokuen. Singles from ¥3,300, twins from ¥3,800.

KANAZAWA EATS & DRINKS

❽ **Tsubajin**（つば甚 寺町5-1-8, Tel.(0762)41-2181）
Jibuni, a stew made with chicken stock, is the specialty. A great winter warmer-upper in this snowy region. Courses from ¥4,000. 11 a.m. to 10 p.m.
❾ **Goriya**（ごり屋 常盤60, Tel.(0762)52-2288）
As the name implies, the river fish known as *gori* is dished out here. ¥3,500. 11:30 a.m. to 7 p.m.

⑩ Miyoshian (三芳庵 兼六町1-11, Tel. (0762)21-0127)
Right in Kenrokuen, this famous place offers *kabura zushi*, fermented turnips and yellow tail fish layered with rice. Tastes better than it sounds. ¥1,000 up. 9 a.m. to 5 p.m., closed Tues.

⑪ Maison de France
(メゾン・ド・フランス 金沢名鉄丸越デパート, Tel.(0762)60-1454)
On the second floor of the Meitetsu Marukoshi Department Store, the famous Japanese *chanson* singer Yoshiko Ishii offers French style omelettes. 10 a.m. to 6 p.m., closed Thurs.

⑫ Takenoan (竹の庵 香林坊2-12-10, Tel.(0762)61-3393)
Kanazawa's best noodles, the locals insist. All home-made. Try their *tempura zaru soba* (cold buckwheat noodles with tempura on top) for ¥850 in the summer.

⑬ Taka-no-ha (鷹の羽 兼六2-20兼六園店, 片町2-2-20片町店,
Tel. (0762)21-2118)
Inexpensive *jibuni* at two locations — one near Kenrokuen, the other in the Katamachi shopping area. ¥800-¥2,000. 11 a.m.-9 p.m.

KANAZAWA SHOPPING

⑭ Moroeya (諸江屋 片町1-3-22)
Probably the best selection of Kutani ware in town, with a museum-like third floor. They'll pack and ship. From ¥1,000 up, up and up. 9 a.m. to 8 p.m., closed Wed.

⑮ Nakajima Menya (中島めんや 尾張町2-2)
The oldest toy store in the area, with dolls of the region. 9 a.m. to 6 p.m., closed Thurs.

⑯ Choami Ohi Pottery (大樋長阿弥 大手町9-19)
Specializing in the strange orange and green tone Ohi ceramics, of course. Nice selection, reasonable prices.

⑰ Morihachi (森八 尾張町2-12-1)
A famous Japanese cake shop with a 300-year history. Beautifully wrapped, fascinatingly crafted cakes, mostly made with sweet beans to eat with green tea. Nice gift for a Japanese friend. ¥1,000 up. 9 a.m. to 7:30 p.m., closed 1st and 3rd Sun.

SENDAI

SENDAI: NORTHERN GATEWAY

The time was when Sendai seemed like the end of the world to Kanto and Kansai residents, let alone foreign visitors. Now the city can be reached in two hours from Omiya, a northern suburb of Tokyo, by the Tohoku Shinkansen *Yamabiko* (¥8,000), making this attractive city and its nearby Matsushima seascapes, mountain scenery and historic spots at last easily accessible.

This is the Tohoku region's capital — the place where people from northern Honshu come to shop, do business and be entertained. It's also an important educational center, seat of Tohoku University. Around the station it looks like all Japanese cities of similar size (population about 600,000). But unlike many of Japan's cities that were fire-bombed during the war, Sendai has made some effort to beautify, at least in the city center. Aoba Dori, Hirose Dori and Jozenji Dori — three main avenues between the Station and the Hirose River — are tree-lined parkways spreading a canopy of green leaves over the passersby.

The greenery, if not always on the streets, is never far away. A high, thickly-wooded ridge — site of the former Aoba castle — dominates to the west beyond the river. From some spots in the city higher mountains can be seen to the south, west and north. On a clear day you can see Matsushima Bay's pine-clad islets to the east from the city's high points.

Sendai is another *jokamachi* (castle town) — this one

once dominated by one of Japan's most powerful feudal lords during the early Tokugawa era, Masamune Date (pronounced dah-tay). The Date clan traces its origins way back to the 12th century, but they remained small-time until the ninth lord Masamune had the good sense to side with Toyotomi Hideyoshi and Ieyasu Tokugawa, the *Shogun* for whom the Tokugawa era is named. As a reward for helping in battle, Ieyasu gave Date permission to build a fine castle. Masamune finally chose Aobayama, a steep hill above the Hirose River in Sendai, as the spot.

Relations with Ieyasu were strained thereafter. Like Maeda in Kanazawa, Date was an outside lord. Ieyasu was forever suspicious of him, as his feif was far from Edo and impossible to control. The policy of permitting powerful outside *daimyo* to build fine castles was calculated to keep them poor. The lords were also required to keep grand estates in Edo, where their wives and first sons were forced to live. Should the outside lords start an uprising, their families would be held in Edo as hostages.

Practically every famous spot in Sendai and nearby Matsushima is connected with the Date clan. **Aoba castle** is gone, destroyed by Meiji forces in 1875, but visitors still climb Aobayama to see the remaining stone walls, a statue of Masamune on horseback — and a fine view of the city and Pacific Ocean. Masamune looks out over Sendai with his good left eye: He lost the use of his right eye as the result of childhood smallpox.

More Masamune mementos lie below Aobayama. Just below is the **Sendai City Museum** (¥200, 9 a.m.-4 p.m., closed Mon.) with a collection of Date family heirlooms, when the building isn't housing a special exhibition. On a small hill called Kyōgamine to the right, Masamune, along with Tadamune and Tsudamune who followed him, are buried. Each has his own small mausoleum, with Masamune's, known as **Zuihoden** (9 a.m.-4 p.m., ¥250), being the most elaborate. The original was destroyed in the air raids of World War II. An elaborate replica, the brilliant gold metalwork and brightly colored bas reliefs decorating the roof beams contrasting sharply with the black lacquer walls, now stands on the site.

Northwest of the business center high on another hill is the **Ōsaki Hachiman Shrine**, the Sendai version of the shrine dedicated to the god of war popular with Japan's military generals during its feudal era. Like the Zuihoden — only this is an original — Ōsaki Hachiman is a fine sample of Momoyama style architecture — the black lacquer, faded gold and bright red, green and blue reminiscent of the Tokugawa's mausoleums at Nikko.

Not far from Ōsaki Hachiman on Kitayama (north

mountain) is **Rinnōji**, Sendai's finest Buddhist temple.
It was rebuilt to commemorate the 250th anniversary of
the death of the wife of an early Date leader after being
destroyed by a fire in 1691. Today only the Nio gate dates
from the period. The temple boasts one of the finest stroll
gardens in northern Japan, which you enter at the right side
of the main hall by a turnstile after depositing a ¥100 coin.
There's something special here in every season — azaleas
and peonies in May, iris in June, maple leaves in October,
pines draped in snow in the winter.

Since the city was badly damaged in the War, Sendai is
essentially new. If the names of the department stores and

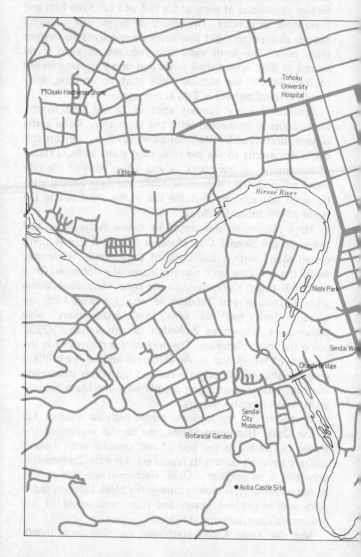

specialty shops look familiar, it's because many of them are from Tokyo. What to look for in Sendai are Tohoku's *kokeshi* wooden dolls — mere wooden cylinders with round heads — made in a number of different villages in the region. Experts can tell in which village the *kokeshi* were made by their shape and painted decorations. Some of the shops specializing in *kokeshi* are listed below. Marumitsu Department Store in front of Sendai Station also has a good selection on its first floor.

Kōtōdai Park, steps from the city's shopping area and in the shadow of the city and prefectural offices, is a popular gathering place for noon-time brown-baggers and families

on weekends. Visitors with more time will want to stroll through **Nishi (west) Park**, just west of the business district and affording fine views out over the Hirose River gorge and up to Aobayama.

Sendai's night town is **Kokubuncho**, and a bustling spot it is after the sun sets. Along Kokubuncho Dori and its side streets are the snack bars, cabarets, coffee shops and restaurants common to all Japanese cities. Some of the more characteristic places with Tohoku flavor — generally more wild and wooly than in other parts of the country — are listed below. When you've had your last drink, buy an ear of corn brushed with soy sauce and roasted over a charcoal fire off the back of one of the trucks that line the street.

The Sendai environs' prime attraction is **Matsushima Bay** dotted with tiny islands on which fine specimens of wind-gnarled Japanese red pine cling. Considered by the Japanese as one of the country's three grand scenic sights, this is the Japanese seascape every foreigner imagines, but not many see. More, it's relatively unspoiled. **Matsushima Kaigan**, the resort center of the area, has so far been spared the ugly concrete buildings that blight the average resort area. You can spend a delightful day here viewing the little islands from both the surrounding well-maintained shoreline and from the deck of the sightseeing boats which navigate the waters.

Godaido, a tiny temple on an island just offshore and reached by two short bridges, is practically a symbol of Matsushima, and one of the many spots around the seawalk offering views across the water. **Kanrantei** (wave-viewing pavilion), a tea house originally built for Toyotomi Hideyoshi's Fushimi Castle, parts of which you may have seen back in Kyoto, then given to Masamune Date and moved to his Edo home and finally moved to Matsushima by Tadamune, sits on a rocky cliff above the sea. It's another example of Momoyama period architecture, and may be the largest tea house surviving from the period (¥150, 7:30 a.m.-5:30 p.m., Apr.-Oct.; 8:30 a.m.-4:30 p.m., Nov.-Mar.).

Zuiganji also has several buildings typical of the flamboyant Momoyama period, four of them "National Treasures". This was originally a temple of the Buddhist Tendai sect which played a role in much of Kyoto's history, but it's been a monastery of the Zen Rinzai sect for the past seven centuries. Masamune Date had the temple rebuilt at the beginning of the 17th century. In addition to the handsome buildings themselves, there are also some fine paintings on sliding doors by popular Kano school painters of the Tokugawa period in the main hall *(Hondo)*. In front of the Hondo are two plum trees — one with pink and the other with white blossoms in late February-early March — brought from Korea after the unsuccessful campaign to capture the country by Hideyoshi, Maeda and Date in 1592 (¥330, 8:30 a.m.-5 p.m., Apr.-Oct.; 9 a.m.-4:30 p.m., Nov.-Mar.).

Two small islands at either end of the town's seawalk — **Oshima** to the south and **Fukurajima** to the east of Godaido — are reached from the mainland by foot bridges and offer more viewing possibilities. Years ago the Japanese, with their passion for organizing and naming every natural sight, decreed four choice vantage points from which to gaze in wonder at the Bay. They are Tomiyama's **Daigyoji Temple, Otakamori** on Miyato Island, **Tamonzan** on Cape Yogasaki and — closest to Matsushima Kaigan — **Ogidani.**

Daigyoji is a 10-minute walk from Rijuzen-Tomiyama Station, just 10-minutes by JNR's Senseki Line east of Matsushima Kaigan; Otakamori is reached by boat in about one hour from either Matsushima Kaigan or Shiogama, Sendai's port; Tamonzan by boat from Shiogama harbor near Hon Shiogama Station on JNR's Senseki Line; and Ogidani is just a 10-minute bus ride or a 25-minute walk from Matsushima Kaigan.

A boat ride is recommended for a look at the islands further offshore. There are a number of small sightseeing boats seating from six to 15 people which offer 15, 30 or 60-minute pleasure cruises in the immediate vicinity. The larger Marubun Matsushima Kissen or Matsushima Wan Kanko Kisen ferries offer one-hour services between Matsushima Kaigan and Shiogama.

The ferry is recommended at least one way between the two towns as an alternate to the train and a chance to see

Ōsaki Hachiman Shrine (Sendai)

some of the islands not easily seen from the mainland. The boats operate regularly between 7:45 a.m. and 4 p.m. from both harbors with fares from ¥1,200 to ¥2,400. Tickets are available from a booth outside Matsushima Kaigan Station or from the individual companies on the town's seawalk.

If you want to stay in one of the Japanese-style hotels in the area, you can make arrangements at the hotel desk outside the Station. Just tell them, or write the price you want to pay, and they'll do the searching by phone.

Should you find it difficult to leave pretty Matsushima Kaigan, venture further east to **Ojika (big deer) Peninsula** and **Kinkazan Island** at its tip for more of this choice section of Japan's Pacific coastline. There's a toll road over Ojika's mountainous spine, or a slower prefectural road which hugs the west coast above coves bobbing with small fishing boats all the way down to Ayukawa village. From Ayukawa it's just a 25-minute Suzuyoshi Kisen ferry ride (¥580) around the tip of the Peninsula to Kinkazan, an unspoiled mountaintop rising out of the sea. No cars are allowed here, and deer and monkeys roam free. Kogane-yama Shrine sits on one side of the mountain and offers sparse but low-priced accommodations. The Kinkazan Kanko Hotel ((02254) 5-2307) offers a little more luxury. There's also a Youth Hostel ((02254) 5-2301) for the bare-bones treatment.

Ayukawa is best reached by Miyagi Kotsu Bus from Ishinomaki Station, a 45-minute ride on JNR's Senseki Line east from Matsushima Kaigan (¥380). There are seven buses per day between 7 a.m. and 5:45 p.m., and the trip takes 1 hour 45 minutes, costs ¥1,150.

The tiny village of **Tsukinoura** on Ojika claims fame to one of the more peculiar chapters in Japan's peculiar history. On September 15, 1613, one Hasekura Rokuemon

Rinnōji Temple (Sendai)

Tsunenaga, accompanied by several Catholic foreign priests, a Spaniard, 180 Japanese sailors and some merchants set sail from the port in a small galleon named the San Juan Baptista for Mexico, Spain and ultimately Rome to visit Pope Paul V under orders from Masamune Date and with the permission of Ieyasu Tokugawa.

Why the voyage was risked remains a mystery. Masamune appeared to have some interest in Christianity, true. Most historians believe the adventurous journey was made in the interest of establishing trade. Hasekura and some of his men made it to the Pope's throne — and quite a swash they cut in Europe, too — to return to Sendai in 1620 only to discover that Tokugawa attitudes toward both Christianity and foreign trade had taken a decidedly negative turn.

Tohoku's most glittering man-made wonder is the celebrated **Konjikidō** (golden hall) of **Chūsonji Temple** in **Hiraizumi**, a small, farming community that was the capital of the region in the 11th century under the Fujiwara family.

Just 17 feet by 17 feet in size, the tiny hall was originally coated with black lacquer and plated with gold panned from nearby rivers. The interior contains three gold altars under which are the remains of the Fujiwara leaders Kiyohira, Motohira and Hidehira. The main pillars are lacquered and inlaid with mother of pearl.

Konjikidō has been restored in recent years and now dazzles the eye more than ever, though you'll have to content yourself with peeking at it through a plate glass window. The mausoleum is protected inside a concrete building. The ¥500 admission fee also entitles you to see the treasures inside the Sankozo, including three large Buddha images, just below, and the Kyozo (sutra hall), a 12th century structure just above Konjikidō. Adjacent to these buildings is one of the few remaining outdoor Noh theaters in all Japan, and it's still used for performances.

All these buildings are part of a temple complex known as Chūsonji, buried beneath ancient cedar *(sugi)* trees on a steep hill above the surrounding rice paddies. Japan's great 17th century *haiku* poet Bashō during his travels to the north paused here, and you can have a cup of green powdered tea and a sweet bean cake on the spot where he stopped for ¥400. Bashō's Tohoku journey tales "The Narrow Road to the Deep North" have been translated into English and make a fine travel companion while touring the area (see Bibliography).

Reflecting on the Fujiwara family's past glory, Bashō wrote, " . . . When a country is defeated, there remain only mountains and rivers, and on a ruined castle in spring only grasses thrive. I sat down on my hat and wept bitterly till I almost forgot time.

> A thicket of summer grass
> Is all that remains
> Of the dreams and ambitions
> Of ancient warriors."

While in Hiraizumi, one more temple is worth your time. It's called **Mōtsuji,** and although nothing but mounds remain where temple buildings once stood, a fine garden, brilliant with iris in late May, surrounding a sizeable pond offers a chance to see one of the few remaining pleasure spots of the elite from the 11th century in Japan. The nobles used to ride in small boats on the lake, replicas of which are anchored mid-pond. The museum holds objects from the Fujiwara family's collection — lacquer ware, iron ware and some scrolls. Admission to the temple grounds and museum is ¥310.

It is just 1 hour 15-minutes from Sendai by express train direct to Hiraizumi Station (¥2,300), or you can take the Tohoku Shinkansen *Yamabiko* to Ichinoseki (about 30 min., ¥3,160), then an Iwate Ken Kotsu Bus direct to Chūsonji (20 min., ¥260).

While in the area, for a greater sampling of the peaceful country scenery, take another Iwate Ken Kotsu Bus from Ichinoseki Station to **Geibikei Gorge** (45 min., ¥470). From the bus stop walk downhill along the banks of the Satetsu River a few minutes to the Geibikei Kanko Center which operates a pleasant 1-hour 30-minute cruise in a flat-bottomed boat up the river and back through a magnificent gorge of granite cliffs. Passengers slip off their shoes after entering the craft, then sit down on grass mats on the boat's bottom. The boat stops briefly and passengers alight for a quick look at the gorge's further reaches by foot, then return in the same boat, serenaded by the oarman enroute. Several departures between 8:30 a.m. and 4:30 p.m., ¥700. Very special.

Matsushima and Chūsonji are the must-see attractions of Tohoku. Those with more time will no doubt want to experience at least one of the many hot springs (*onsen*) in the region. The *onsen* here have not completely escaped the tacky development that's spoiled most mountain resorts since World War II. But there is a better chance of finding the hot spring of your dreams in Tohoku than in any other part of the country. Mixed bathing is also more common here than in any other region, albeit, no Japanese woman under 60 would think of crawling into a tub with a bunch of strange men. Voyeurs be warned.

The *onsen* village of **Narugo** might be your perfect choice. The town hasn't escaped modern intrusions, including a few high-rise eyesores. But there are plenty of low-rise inns here proud of their past and determined to maintain the old traditions. Yusaya (ゆさや, tel. (02298)3-2565) has just 17 rooms and prides itself on offering cuisine typical of the region for from ¥7,000 to ¥10,000 per person with two meals. Owner Masanobu Yusa, who traces his family of inn-keepers back some 400 years, speaks English and is pleased to entertain foreign guests with tales of the area.

Just beside Yusaya is the village's public bath **Takinoyu** where for ¥100 you can relax in a cypress tub filled with milky sulphurous water which drips from a log connected to a spring outside. The bath's high roof is open to the outdoors under the eaves. People have been bathing on the spot since the year 837.

Like many *onsen* in the Tohoku area, Narugo is also famous for the *kokeshi* dolls made here. Some 70 craftsmen are still at work, and a few of them ply their trade in the windows of the shops along the streets. Narugo *kokeshi* are distinguished by their concave bodies, red flower designs and a head that squeaks when it turns. The sound resembles the cry of a small bird (in Japanese, *narugo*). At the **Nippon Kokeshi Kan** (¥150, 8:30 a.m.-5:30 p.m., Apr.-Oct.) some 3,000 *kokeshi* from all over Japan are displayed.

The nearby village of **Iwadeyama** was home to Masamune Date for a few years before he built Aobajo at Sendai. Predictably, the castle is gone from the hill on which it sat. But the hill is still there, and from the park on top there is a fine view of the rice paddies and mountains beyond. Just below the hill is a classic 17th century home built originally as temporary quarters for Masamune's

Geibikei Gorge

fourth son Muneyasu after the castle on the hill burned down in 1663. When a new castle was built, the home became a school used by the children of the lord's retainers to study Chinese classics. It's called **Yubikan**, and you can still visit the home and a handsome stroll-type garden added at the beginning of the 18th century (¥200). The thatched-roof house is the oldest of its type in the country and offers great solace, if you can escape the groups of school children who descend regularly. Iwadeyama is also known for its bamboo basketware, a natural outcome of having a number of lush bamboo groves in its midst.

There are direct JNR trains from Sendai to Iwadeyama and Narugo (about two hours, ¥1,130). You can also take the Tohoku Shinkansen *Yamabiko* to Furukawa (20 min., ¥1,370), then change for a local train to Iwadeyama or Narugo (40 min., ¥440). The two towns are about 30 minutes apart by train.

If you long for the Tohoku *onsen* experience and have less time on your hands, you might catch the train in Sendai for Sakunami (40 min., ¥380), from where it's a short bus ride to **Sakunami Onsen**, site of a few hotels along a river bank in a mountain valley. There's no public bath here. If you are not a guest at one of the hotels, you might plead with the man at the front desk of Iwamatsu Ryokan (free minibus service from Sakunami Station) to let you use the hotel's outdoor bath at the bottom of the ravine. If the hotel's not crowded with guests, they may let you use their *rotenburo* (outdoor bath) for a small fee. There's a bus stop in front of the *ryokan* for a Sendai Shi Kotsu Kyoku Bus back to Sendai Station (about 1 hour, ¥740).

You can easily combine Sakunami with **Yamadera**, the next express train stop from Sakunami (about 30 min., ¥240). As the name in Japanese implies, this is a mountain *(yama)* temple *(dera (tera))*, (also known as Risshakuji) — and what a mountain. The steps from the bottom near the station appear to go right up to Buddhist heaven, with many small temple buildings and alternate paths along the way to divert you from ever climbing all the way to the top. This temple started out in the year 860 as a northern branch of the famed Enryakuji Temple you met back on Mt. Hiei in Kyoto, but fell to hard times during the bloody fighting during the 14th-16th centuries and was built again in the early Tokugawa period. Yamadera's most famous visitor was that inveterate traveler, the poet Bashō, who stopped here in 1689 and wrote an arresting few lines about the Japanese cicada whose incessant screeching in the late summer induces insomnia. To the Japanese, it's something akin to music, however. Wrote Bashō:

> "In the utter silence
> Of a temple,
> A cicada's voice alone
> Penetrates the rocks."

Sendai and its neighboring attractions are well outlined in an excellent English guide book titled simply "**Sendai**" and written by three American residents. (See Bibliography). Curiously, this book is easier to find in Tokyo's English language bookstores than it is in Sendai. Buy before you head north.

SENDAI SLEEPING

❶ Hotel Rich Sendai （ホテルリッチ仙台）
2-2-2 Kokunbuncho, (0222)62-8811. Smack in the heart of swinging Kokunbuncho for late-night pub crawling. Nothing fancy here, but handy. One of a chain. Singles from ¥4,600, twins from ¥10,000.

❷ Mitsui Urban Hotel Sendai （三井アーバンホテル仙台）
2-18-11 Honmachi, (0222)65-3131. Another marvel of efficiency in tiny spaces, designed for those tiny businessmen. New. Overlooks pretty Kōtōdai Park. Singles from ¥4,500, twins from ¥10,000.

❸ Hotel Koyo （ホテル江陽）
7-1-4 Ichibancho, (0222)62-6311. A French *fin de siecle* interior in — Sendai? Yes, and not to be believed. Look at the lobby and decide about the rooms for yourself. Singles from ¥5,000, twins from ¥11,000.

❹ Tokyo Dai-Ichi Hotel Sendai （東京第一ホテル仙台）
2-3-18 Chuo, (0222)62-1355. Another business hotel, one of a chain, without any pretensions. Handy to shopping, the tourist spots. Singles from ¥4,500, twins from ¥8,800.

❺ Sendai Tokyu Hotel （仙台東急ホテル）
2-9-25 Ichibancho, (0222)62-2411. Another chain member, but a notch above the usual business hotel in both facilities — and prices. New, with the usual Japanese-Las Vegas-style flash. Singles from ¥6,500, twins from ¥11,000.

❻ Sendai Pacific Hotel （仙台パシフィックホテル）
1-3-12 Chuo, (0222)63-6611. Practically on top of Sendai Station, so you can leap out of bed and be on a train to the area's seashore and mountains in a jiffy. Singles from ¥4,400, twins from ¥8,000.

❼ Sendai Washington Hotel, Washington Hotel II
（仙台ワシントンホテル）
2-3-1 Omachi, (0222)22-2111. Another chain product, right on

pretty Aoba Dori, handy to Nishi Park and Aobayama. Singles from ¥4,000, twins from ¥7,000; in the new annex across the street, singles from ¥5,000, twins from ¥8,000.

SENDAI EATS & DRINKS

❽ Robata (炉ばた 国分町2-5-12, Tel. (0222)23-0316, 国分町2-4-17, Tel. (0222)22-3533)

A real Sendai experience, but not for the squeamish. No menu. Tell the man or woman on the tatami mat behind the counter what you want to drink (beer, sake or *nigori-zake*, a thick and unrefined rice-gruel sake common to Tohoku). With the drink you'll automatically get a tray of pickled vegetables to help work up your thirst. The "fish of the day" are listed on the wall (in Japanese, of course). Try *hoya*, a bright orange, bumpy sea creature whose soft insides you scoop out with a spoon; or fresh *nishin* (herring) brushed with soy sauce and grilled over an open fire. You sit at a counter behind which the master sits in front of a fireplace sunk into the floor. Folk art decorates the walls and shelves, including a pair of giant wooden phallic symbols. Two locations just off Kokuncho Dori, a block north of Hotel Rich. This is essentially a drinking place, but you can make a meal with the fish. Average ¥2,000 6-10 p.m.

❾ Matsuribayashi (祭囃子 大町2-7-7, Tel. (0222)64-3205)

Edo-style cooking characteristic of northeastern Japan. The portions are a bit larger, the flavor stronger, with very salty *miso* soup and pickles. Better call in advance for a seat. This cozy little place a couple of blocks north of the Washington Hotel II packs them in. No English menu. Struggle, or grab a passing Japanese on the street for an explanation of the menu posted outside. ¥3,000 range. 5-10:30 p.m. closed Mon., hol.

❿ Yōruka (ヨールカ 国分町3, Tel. (0222)65-4942 中央1-1-1エスパル内, Tel. (0222)67-4088))

Japanese-style Russian food in two locations — The Rich Hotel, and the basement of S-Pal Department Store attached to Sendai Station. Special ¥600 lunch sets are a bargain. More pricey at night with courses from ¥1,300 to ¥8,000. Try their *borscht* soup or a *piroshiki* meat pie. S-Pal, 10 a.m.-9 p.m.; Hotel Rich, 11:30 a.m.-9 a.m.

⓫ Restaurant Rheingold (ラインゴールド 一番町, Tel. (0222)25-8691)

The name and atmosphere — beam ceilings, red brick walls, lantern lights — lead you to believe this is a German restaurant, but the menu puts you back on the track: just more "western style" food. The usual spaghetti, hamburger steak and pilaff dishes. In the evening, fish, pork or beef courses with bread or rice, salad and coffee for between ¥1,500-¥2,500. 11 a.m.-9 p.m.

⓬ Noix (ノワ 八幡3, Tel. (0222)22-1111)

A lovely room with white stucco walls, brick floors, white linen, fresh flowers and a garden outside the front door. Spaghetti, curry rice or pilaff dishes for lunch; cakes and coffee in the afternoon; steaks from ¥2,900 up in the evening. Features the cuisine of one European country for a couple of days each month in special courses at ¥5,000-¥7,000. Handy place for lunch after visiting Ōsaki Hachiman Shrine. Lunch, ¥1,000-¥2,000. 11:30 a.m.-9 p.m.

⓭ Kurumaya (車屋 国分町2-5-17, Tel. (0222)65-1131)

This Japanese restaurant, easily spotted with a waterwheel outside its door, is right on Kokubuncho Dori behind Hotel Rich and features inexpensive *sukiyaki* and *shabu shabu* from ¥2,100. 5-11 p.m.

⑭ Cafe Mozart （カフェ モーツァルト 一番町3-11-14, Tel. (0222)63-4689）
Sendai's classical music buffs flock here for the recorded music and artist's atelier atmosphere. Good coffee and cakes. Third floor of building next door to Jusco Department Store on Ichibancho shopping mall. 10 a.m.-10 p.m.

⑮ Peter Pan （ピーターパン 国分町2-6-1, Tel. (0222)64-1742）
Another third-floor room across the street from Robata's main shop off Kokubuncho Dori. "Rock & Tea Since 1972" says the sign. Coffee or booze and recorded rock music. 12-10 p.m.

⑯ Count （カウント 一番町4-5-42, Tel. (0222)63-0238）
The recorded jazz hear practically blows the roof off this end-of-an-alley room leading off the street running south from the side of Mitsukoshi Department Store. Owner has a huge collection of Count Basey records, thus the name. 12-11 p.m.

⑰ Pepe Gonzalez （ペペ 国分町2-5, Tel. (0222)63-7806, 一番町, Tel. (0222)64-2785）
A drinking spot with Mexican snacks such as *tacos, enchiladas* and *chili rellenos* in two locations: one is in the Goroku Building just behind Hotel Rich on the 4th floor; the other near Mitsukoshi. 5 p.m.-2-3 a.m.

⑱ Orgel （オルゴール 大町2-11-7, Tel. (0222)23-8280）
"Coffee & Goods Orgel" says the neon sign plastered across the front of this cozy coffee shop near Nishi Park. A good place to plop after climbing Aobayama. 10 a.m.-7:30 p.m.

SENDAI SHOPPING

What to buy after *kokeshi*? The craft shops have other folk art from the Tohoku area. Sendai chests *(tansu)* are considered the best in Japan, and you can see the new ones in department stores. The old ones are becoming scarce. *Hira* cloth wallets, made from a kind of hemp, wear forever. The local lacquer ware, deep red and durable even in dry climates, is called *tamamushi-nuri*. Typical ceramics include *tsutsumi-yaki*, with a creamy underglaze plus an overglaze in a different color, from Miyagi Prefecture; *Soma-Koma-yaki*, easy to recognize with its prancing horse patterns, from Fukushima Prefecture; and *Hirashimizu-yaki*, much prized for its simple tan and brown-spotted surfaces, from Yamagata Prefecture.

⑲ Shimanuki （しまぬき 一番町3）
A wide assortment of *kokeshi*, plus other Tohoku folk art in two locations: on the Chuo Dori shopping mall near Fujisaki Department Store, and in the basement of S-Pal attached to Sendai Station. 9:30 a.m.-7:30 p.m., closed second Thurs.

⑳ Ganguan Kokeshiya （玩愚庵こけし屋 国分町1-6-3）
Kokeshi exclusively, and lots to pick from. Just off Kokubuncho Dori across from "Cake & Tea Kenzo," a block south of Hotel Rich. 8 a.m.-7 p.m.

㉑ Kōgensha （光原社 一番町1-4-10）
Quality folk art from all over Japan, plus a few other Asian countries. Two blocks south of Aoba Dori on Kokubuncho Dori. 10 a.m.-6:30 p.m.

㉒ Craft Corner （クラフトコーナー 中央2-4-8）
More folk art, but some trendy, modern crafts here as well. On Chuo Dori shopping mall behind Daiei Dept .

NAGASAKI

長崎

NAGASAKI: PEEPHOLE TO OUTSIDE

Although a thoroughly Japanese city to a foreigner's eye at this time in its history, Nagasaki stirs visions of exoticism in the Japanese. During the Tokugawa period it was the only port where foreign trade was legally allowed. The Dutch, because they were less zealous for the Christian faith, were given permission to do business from a tiny, fan-shaped island connected by causeway to the mainland. There was also a Chinese colony, since they had been visiting the port for many years. Shortly after the Jesuit missionary St. Francis Xavier arrived at an island off southern Kyushu in 1549, the Jesuits founded a Christian stronghold at Nagasaki which was not entirely stamped out even during the purge by the Tokugawas. Finally, this city, along with Hiroshima, was the target of the world's second atomic bomb attack on August 9, 1945.

Hints of all this remain, but what will strike you most is Nagasaki's lovely setting on steep mountains which rise above a narrow harbor leading to the open sea. The Madame Butterfly legend, basis for the Puccini opera, is simply nonsense. But if it never really happened, it surely could have, in this, perhaps the most romantic city in all Japan. The Japanese play the story to the hilt. The **Glover Mansion** (¥600, 8 a.m. to 6 p.m.; Dec.-Feb., 8:30 a.m.-5 p.m.), a Victorian home once owned by a British merchant, has been moved up on to *Orandazaka* (Holland Hill) with a splendid view of the harbor and city. You're carried up a moving sidewalk to the residence, from where you descend to a series of terraces in a plastic imitation of an Italian villa. If it's all too much, cast your eyes on the view and try to forget the madness behind.

Adjacent is the **Oura Catholic Church** (¥200, 8 a.m. to 5 p.m.), built in Gothic style in 1865 to commemorate the death of 26 Christian martyrs in 1597. The site of the killings is across the valley on a hillside just above Nagasaki Station. It's now known as **Nishizaka Park** and contains the **26 Saints Martyrdom Memorial Hall** (¥150, 9 a.m. to 6 p.m.; Dec.-Feb., 5 p.m.), and a chapel with twin towers reminiscent of Gaudi's Sagrada Familia in Barcelona. Six foreign and 20 Japanese Christians died here after refusing to give up their faith on demand of Hideyoshi who banned Christianity in 1597. According to legend, the men looked like sleeping angels while hanging on their crosses for 80 days after the crucifixion, and during the period many miracles occurred. Christians from all over Japan gather here each February 5, the date of the execution.

Besides Christianity, the Portuguese missionaries' chief import may have been a tasty sponge cake named *kasutera*, believed to come from the Portuguese word *castella*, and *pan*, now the Japanese borrowed word for bread. No Japanese visits Nagasaki without lugging home boxes of *kasutera* for friends and relatives as souvenirs. **Fukusaya** (8:30 a.m. to 8 p.m., closed Mon.), with their main shop near Shianbashi, is the most famous brand.

Since the great Chinese port of Shanghai is barely 900 miles across the East China Sea from Nagasaki, the links between the two ports are centuries old. The Chinese being the only other foreigners allowed in Nagasaki besides the Dutch during the Tokugawa era, a sizeable Chinatown sprang up in the city's heart. **Kofukuji Temple** was established by the Chinese residents, and its third abbot, Itsunen, introduced Chinese painting to the city in the 17th century.

Just above the business center, **Sofukuji Temple** has a gate tower built in the architectural style of the late Ming Dynasty. Like Kofukuji, this temple also had a Chinese priest as its first abbot. Both belong to the Obaku sect of Zen Buddhism. Just up the Nakajima River from the shopping area is **Meganebashi** (glasses bridge), built by the second abbot of Kofukuji in traditional Chinese style. The two arches are reflected in the water to form what looks like a pair of spectacles.

For those interested in what happened on August 9, 1945, you'll want to visit the **International Cultural Hall** (¥50, 9 a.m. to 5 p.m.) at Peace Park in Hamaguchimachi. The museum here is perhaps not as impressive as the one at

Hiroshima, but it better explains the human misery of the world-altering event. Some 75,000 people died from the Nagasaki atomic blast.

Nearby **Urakami Catholic Church**, rebuilt in 1959 after being destroyed by the bomb, is situated in a neighborhood where Christianity survived the persecutions under the Tokugawas and many Christians here admitted their faith again after the Meiji Restoration.

Save for a few wooden buildings, one of which houses the **Nagasaki Municipal Museum** with objects from the Dutch colony on view (9 a.m. to 5 p.m., closed Mon.), there is little left of Dejima, the island where the Dutch traders were kept under surveillance. Due to land fill, it's no longer an island but part of the dock area next to the

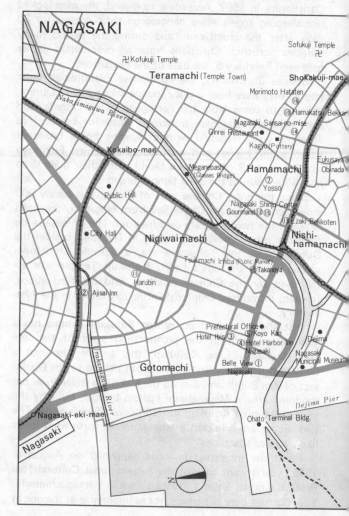

harbor. Although its building doesn't date from the Tokugawa era, **Ginrei Restaurant** (10 a.m. to 9 p.m., ¥3,500-¥6,000, Tel. (0958)21-2073) in the business center is very "Amsterdam", with a fine collection of Dutch china and glass, not to mention what's probably the best beef in the city.

For an interesting overall view from the hills above, take the #3 streetcar to the end of the line deep into the valley in which Nagasaki is built and walk uphill on the right to the local **"temple town"**. From the path there are fine views across the city and you'll pass Kofukuji Temple and finally drop back into the shopping area.

Possibilities for trips outside waterbound Nagasaki always involve the sea. No matter which way you head,

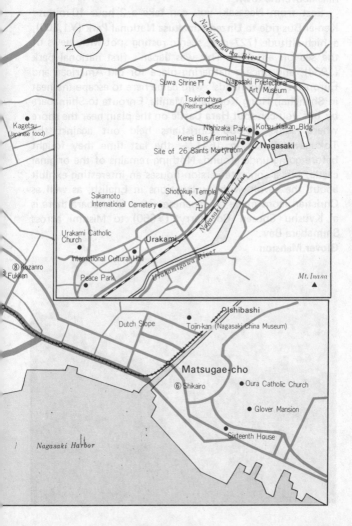

you'll be skirting a shore, or if you go by ferry, over the waves. A two-hour Ken-ei Bus ride from the terminal of the same name across from Nagasaki Station will bring you to **Sasebo** (¥1,100), built along the shores of Omura Bay. Take a 30-minute bus ride from the bus terminal in front of Sasebo Station to Kashimae (¥180), where you can catch a Kobaruto Line boat to **Hirado**. The slower, 1-hour 30-minute boat (¥1,000) is recommended. This large island off the west coast of Kyushu also has links with British, Dutch and Chinese traders. The small village has several *minshuku*, a rebuilt castle at the harbor entrance, a fine museum of art objects belonging to the local *daimyo*, another Catholic church associated with the islands Christian history and quiet pedestrian pathways winding over the hills above the town.

East from Nagasaki you can take a 2 hour 10-minute Ken-ei Bus ride to **Unzen-Amakusa National Park** (¥1,300), a high-altitude (727 m.), scenic resting spot with views of the sea on all sides. This was Japan's first national park (1934), and once a gathering place for old American and European "China hands" who came here to escape the heat in Shanghai, Hong Kong and Manila. Enroute to Shimabara by bus you can spot **Hara Castle** on the plain near the shore where some 30,000 Christians held out against the Tokugawa forces in 1641 — the last time they fought before going underground. Nothing remains of the original castle, but a concrete version houses an interesting exhibit about the revolt with explanations in English, as well as Christian icons made by Japanese. From Shimabara there is a Kyushu Shosen Co. ferry (¥660) to Misumi across Shimabara Bay.

Glover Mansion

NAGASAKI SLEEPING

❶ Belle View Nagasaki （ホテルベルビュー長崎）
Edo machi 1-25 (0958)22-0019. Comfortable, and a handy location.
Singles ¥4,000, twins ¥8,500, with breakfast.

❷ Ajisai Inn Nagasaki （あじさいイン長崎）
Ebisu machi 4-5 (0958)22-7771. In center, and convenient to public
transport. Singles ¥3,900, twins ¥6,500.

❸ Hotel Ibis （ホテルアイビス）
Kabashima machi 8-19 (0958)24-2171. Singles ¥4,400, twins
¥8,800.

❹ Hotel Harbor Inn Nagasaki （ホテルハーバーイン長崎）
Kabashima machi 8-17 (0958)27-1111. Singles ¥4,300, twins
¥7,700.

❺ Koyo Kan Business Hotel （港洋館ビジネスホテル）
Kabashima machi 7-9 (0958)24-2058. Singles ¥3,500, twins ¥6,200.

NAGASAKI EATS & DRINKS

❻ Shikairo （四海楼 松ヶ枝町4-5, Tel. (0958)24-4744）
This is one of Japan's best Chinese restaurants, once frequented by
the Chinese students who used to go to school here. The grandfather of the present manager invented a local specialty known as
Nagasaki *champon,* a hearty noodle dish. From 1899. 11 a.m.-
7 p.m.

❼ Yosso （吉宗 浜町8-9, Tel. (0958)21-0001）
Another old restaurant (1866) which specializes in an egg custard
flecked with mushrooms and vegetables and oozing a fishy taste and
smell *(chawan mushi)*. Also slightly steamed fish. 11 a.m.-8:30 p.m.,
closed Tues.

❽ Kozanro （江山楼 新地12-2, Tel. (0958)21-3735）
More *champon* in what was once Chinatown. ¥400-¥1,000. 11 a.m.-
9 p.m.

❾ Obinada （オビナダ 船大工町3, Tel. (0958)24-1437）
Italian dishes from a low ¥450 in a spot popular with young
foreigners.

❿ Hamakatsu Bekkan
（浜勝別館 鍛冶屋町6-50, Tel. (0958)23-2193）
Shippoku ryori, a mixture of Chinese, Japanese and western dishes
that originated in Nagasaki, is what draws customers here. Average
¥2,000. 12-11 p.m.

⓫ Harubin （ハルビン 興善町2, Tel. (0958)22-7443）
Russian, as the name implies, with Siberian smoked beef, pork
steak, black bread and vodka for from ¥3,000. 11 a.m.-10 p.m.

⓬ Gourmand （グルマンド 浜の町2-53, Tel. (0958)27-3339）
Home-made French food at a low ¥800 for lunch; ¥3,000 for
dinner.

NAGASAKI SHOPPING

⓭ Ezaki Bekkoten （江崎べっ甲店 魚の町7-13）
Tortoise shell accessories — tie pins, combs, cuff links — are the
specialty. A Nagasaki souvenir favorite. 9 a.m.-8 p.m.

⑭ Nagasaki Sansai-no-mise （長崎三彩の店 油屋町1）
A local porcelain in a combination of three colors. Eguchi Shuzan is the potter. 10 a.m.-8 p.m.

⑮ Nagasaki Shinju Center （長崎真珠センター 浜町3）
Pearls, another local product, in a wide variety. The gold and cream colored pearls are cheaper, pink and white more expensive. 10 a.m.-8 p.m., closed Sun., 1st and 3rd Thurs.

⑯ Morimoto Hataten （森本ハタ店 鍛冶屋町6）
Nagasaki's only kite maker, busy during the city's kite festivals every Sunday and on April 29 and May 3. 8 a.m.-9 p.m.

⑰ Fukusaya （福砂屋 船大工町3-1）
The city's most famous *castella* sponge cake maker.

⑱ Takanoya （高野屋 築町1）
The Japanese line up here for *karasumi*, a cod-roe sausage which is sliced thin before serving.

⑲ Fukken （福建 出島町4-13）
A Chinese sweet shop for lovers of bean jams and sesame seeds.

Sofukuji Temple

SAPPORO

SAPPORO: ORIENTAL KANSAS CITY

You notice the difference not long after you leave Chitose Airport. What Hokkaido has that Japan's other islands don't is space. Also, it has a climate like that of the northern U.S. or central Europe, with vegetation to match: elm trees instead of bamboo, corn and potatoes and dairy cows in dry fields instead of rice paddies. To an American, all this looks vaguely familiar. Maybe you're in Iowa, or Vermont.

Hokkaido is Japan's last frontier. The Ainu, the island's earlier dwellers who once lived by hunting and fishing have, like the American Indians, been all but driven out by their conquerors. What remains of them, especially around the tourist centers, is a pretty sorry sight.

The Japanese, mostly second, third and fourth sons from Honshu's northern provinces, only began migrating to Hokkaido in any number during the past century. Matsumae, one of the Tokugawa's generals, set up a fortress in the port town of the same name in the early 17th century. Hakodate, along with four other ports, was opened to foreigners after Commodore Matthew Perry barged in to demand that Japan be opened to trade in 1854. The government moved to Sapporo in 1871, and that city has taken the lead on the island ever since.

Sapporo is an attractive city of about 1.3 million, and thanks to the influence of American advisors early in its history, it's an easy city in which to get around. The streets

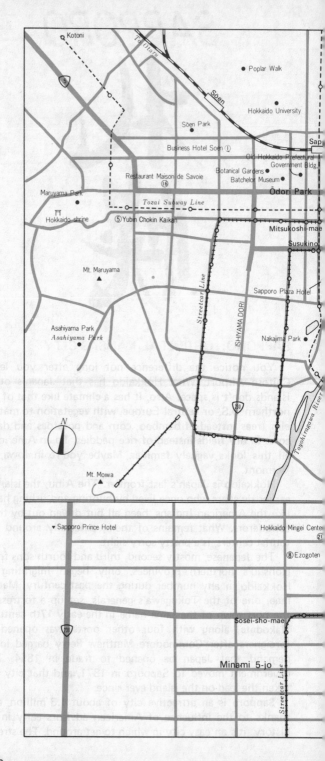

SAPPORO

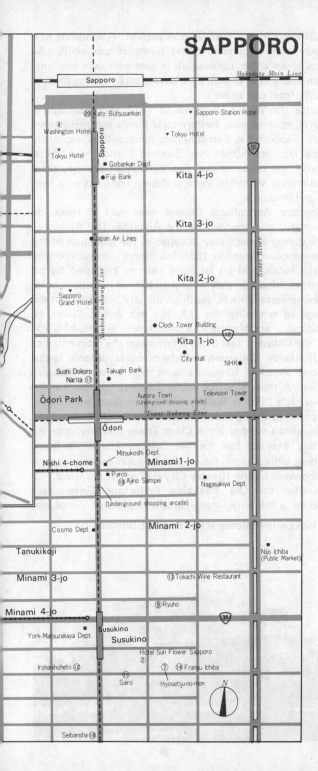

Hakodate Main Line

Sapporo

⑳ Kato Butsusankan ▼ Sapporo Station Hotel

④ Washington Hotel
▼ Tokyu Hotel

Tokyu Hotel

● Gobankan Dept.

Kita 4-jo

● Fuji Bank

Kita 3-jo

● Japan Air Lines

Kita 2-jo

▼ Sapporo Grand Hotel

● Clock Tower Building

Kita 1-jo

● City Hall

NHK ●

Sushi Dokoro Narita ⑰

● Takugin Bank

Ōdori Park

Aurora Town (Underground shopping arcade)

Television Tower

Tozai Subway Line

Ōdori

Mitsukoshi Dept.

Minami 1-jo

Nishi 4-chome

■ Parco
■ Ajino Sampei ⑩

Nagasakiya Dept.

(Underground shopping arcade)

Cosmo Dept. ■

Minami 2-jo

Tanukikoji

Nijo Ichiba (Public Market)

Minami 3-jo

⑬ Tokachi Wine Restaurant

Minami 4-jo

⑨ Ryuho

36

York-Matsuzakaya Dept. ■

Susukino
Susukino

Hotel Sun Flower Sapporo ②

Irohanihoheto ⑫

⑪ Sairo

⑦ ⑭ Fransu Ichiba

Hyosetsu-no-mon

N

Seibansha ⑱

Nanboku Subway Line

Soset River

731

112

Pata Town

143

are laid out in the familiar grid pattern. A sparkling new subway with automated ticket turnstiles can whisk you across town either north-south or east-west over two lines which intersect at **O-dori**, a handsome park running through the city from east to west.

Since the Winter Olympics of 1972 which brought a large number of new, western-style hotels and department stores, Sapporo has a streamlined, modern look, especially in the business district near Sapporo Station — a "Little Tokyo", the residents say. But throughout the city there are surviving Victorian frame buildings right out of a New England landscape.

Sapporo Agricultural College, now part of Hokkaido University, was founded by the American Dr. William S. Clark during a year's stay in Japan at the invitation of the Japanese government in 1876. His memory is much revered by the locals, and his students were so impressed by his Christian influence, they went with him on horseback as far as Shimamatsu, 24 km. south of the city, when he left the college to return to the U.S. His last words, "Boys, be ambitious", are plastered all over town. A bust of Clark, also the College's first dean, is just inside the main entrance to **Hokkaido University** which occupies Japan's largest campus about a 10-minute walk northwest of Sapporo Station. A must stop for young Japanese romantics is the University's **"Poplar Walk"**, a dirt road lined with poplar trees next to the agriculture experimental station.

Sapporo's symbol is the **Clock Tower Building**, once the military exercise hall for the College. The white frame building with a clock tower over its main entrance is now overpowered by the 19-story City Hall across the street.

Nearby the **Old Hokkaido Prefectural Government Building**, a red-brick, many-gabled example of Victoriana,

Old Hokkaido Prefectural Government Building

looms over two lotus ponds set in a small park crowded with munching office workers during the noon hour.

One block west is the handsome **Hokkaido University Botanical Garden** (¥100), a wide expanse of lawns, old trees, azalea and rose gardens with two small museums. The **Batchelor Museum** (¥30) holds a collection of Ainu handicrafts gathered by Dr. John Batchelor, an English minister who lived on Hokkaido. The museum was formerly Batchelor's home. Next door another wooden building displays native stuffed animals and birds — Hokkaido bears, wolves, deer and birds (¥30, closed Mon.).

Sapporo's shopping district stretches from Sapporo Station to Susukino along the wide tree-lined Sapporo Eki-mae Dori. The merchandise is no different than what you saw in Tokyo, except for the souvenir shops well-stocked with grotesque Ainu-style wood carvings — lurking bears with salmon in their mouths being the most popular theme. There are also some rustic local pottery, and an abundance of white chocolate made with milk from Hokkaido's prolific cows.

Stretching underneath Sapporo Eki-mae Dori between the O-dori and Susukino subway stations is **Pole Town**, an underground shopping arcade providing relief during the city's nippy winters.

One of Sapporo's nicest features is its accessibility to the

Lake Mashuko (Akan National Park)

great outdoors. An eight-minute subway ride to Maruyama Park Station will bring you to **Maruyama Park**, a virgin forest covering a perfectly round mountain. You can climb it over a trail which starts behind the Shinto shrine at the base. There are also a zoo and baseball stadium.

The city's closest real mountain is **Moiwa**, just a 25-minute bus ride from Sapporo Station. You can reach the 531 m. summit by a ropeway to an observation platform about half way up, then on foot the rest of the way. If it's clear you can see the Teine, Eniwa and Tarumae mountains to the west, Ishikari Bay to the north and the lofty Daisetsu mountains in the center of Hokkaido to the east.

Nakajima Park is just south of the business district and built between two rivers with a lake, another Victorian gingerbread building now used as a wedding hall, and a tea house — one of the few hints of anything traditionally Japanese in the whole city.

Sapporo is less than an hour from some of the best skiing in all Japan, a fact made known to the world during the Winter Olympics. The **Teine Olympia Ski Grounds**, site of the alpine, bobsled and toboggan events, is just 45 minutes by bus. There is good skiing even closer at Mt. Moiwa and **Mt. Arai**, the latter being the most tame of the slopes.

Susukino is considered one of the liveliest night life quarters in all Japan outside Tokyo, and no man heads for Sapporo from Honshu without being ribbed by his buddies about the neighborhood's pleasures. Some 3,000 bars, cabarets and striptease joints are crammed into this area, and the action goes on well into the early morning hours. A tradition is to wind up the evening with a bowl of Sapporo's own *ramen*, a great bowl of Chinese-style noodles in the sauce of your choice.

Having traveled this far off the beaten tourist track on Honshu, you'll no doubt want to sample some of Hokkaido's scenic attractions which to most people are the prime reason for coming up here. Lakes, smoking volcanoes, deep gorges and rugged coastlines may be seen in the three national parks.

The **Shikotsu-Toya National Park** between Sapporo and Hakodate is easiest to reach for the short-time visitor. A recommended route for an overall view of the park's sights is a trip by Donan or Jotetsu Bus from the terminal beside Sapporo Station to **Toyako Onsen** (¥2,150), a lakeside spa at the foot of a very active volcano named Mt. Usu. The town, like most on this island, is grim, but if you cast your eyes across the lake to Nakanoshima, a mountain in its center, and beyond to Mt. Yotei, you'll be enchanted. For ¥6,000 per person at **Hifumi Ryokan**, a six-story high-rise with Japanese-style rooms, you can enjoy a sizeable room and two very good meals, although there is no view of the lake.

Another 1 hour 40-minute Donan Bus ride from Toyako will bring you to **Noboribetsu** (¥1,000), a spa famous for its variety of mineral waters and the fact that it's one of the few places where men and women still bathe together. But don't over-anticipate. At the **Daiichi Takimoto Hotel** giant, terraced bath (¥800, 7 a.m.-5 p.m.) where everyone gathers, bathing etiquette is meticulously maintained. One must keep one's little towel in its proper place — grandmas and grandpas excepted as they always are in Japan. The town itself is equally as unattractive as Toyako, but the gorge in which it sits is spectacularly covered with a variety of trees. A 10-minute ride by ropeway (¥1,400) will bring you to the top of **Mt. Kuma**, where the ropeway developers have built concrete pits for 70 (count them) very smelly bears and a few thatched Ainu huts for some tourist-conscious Ainu. Incidentally, there is also a nice view of the Pacific and mountain-locked Lake Kuttara below. From Noboribetsu there are buses back to Sapporo, with a stop at Chitose Airport for those returning to Honshu.

Daisetsuzan in Hokkaido's center is the most spectacular of the three national parks, and the largest in Japan, encompassing five peaks over 6,500 ft. It can be reached within two hours from Sapporo by express train to Asahikawa (¥2,500), an ugly industrial city, then by bus (¥1,400) or hired car for another 1 hour 50-minutes to **Sounkyo Onsen**, a spa in a deep canyon which serves as a gateway to the park.

Further east, and a journey requiring several days to do it justice, is **Akan National Park**. It's not as high as Daisetsuzan, but it's equally as rugged and mostly unspoiled with dense forests and three major lakes, Kutcharo being the largest mountain lake in the country. **Lake Akan** boasts the *marimo*, small balls of duckweed which float on the lake's surface and which are found at only two other lakes in the world (one in Switzerland, and one on the Siberian Island of Sakhalin). The most interesting gateway to the park is **Bihoro**, a dirt-street and clapboard town reminiscent of the American West. North of Bihoro is **Abashiri**, a small port town open to the Okhotsk Sea with good beaches, camping sites, a botanical garden, a fine collection of Ainu artifacts in its museum and a jail built like a European castle for the country's most dangerous criminals. The Ainu in and around Akan are still living by hunting and fishing, unlike their brothers at **Shiraoi** which is more frequented by tourists.

If you come by train from Tokyo to Hokkaido, you'll dock at **Hakodate**, the island's second city. Built on hills overlooking the Tsugaru Straits, it's considered one of Japan's three most beautiful cities by night (along with Kobe and Nagasaki). A cable car up **Mt. Hakodate** offers the best view. Adding to the old-fashioned western flavor of the town is the **Japan Orthodox Resurrection Church**, a Byzantine-style edifice, the original of which was founded by a Russian prelate in 1862; and **Goryokaku**, a western-style, massive, star-shaped sandstone fort built for the Island's defense in 1855. At this spot the Tokugawa forces held out against the new Meiji government in 1868.

Sapporo Snow Festival

SAPPORO SLEEPING

❶ Business Hotel Soen (ビジネスホテル桑園)
Kita-Rokujo, Nishi 14-chome, Chuo-ku, (011)231-1661. A short
taxi ride from Sapporo Station. Singles ¥3,400, twins ¥6,800.

❷ Hotel Sun Flower Sapporo (ホテルサンフラワー札幌)
Minami-Gojo, Nishi 3-chome, Chuo-ku, (011)512-5533. Smack in
the heart of swinging Susukino. Singles ¥5,000, twins ¥8,800.

❸ Sapporo Plaza Hotel (札幌プラザホテル)
Minami-Shichijo, Nishi 1-chome, Chuo-ku, (011)511-7211. Five
minutes from Susukino subway station. Singles ¥4,700, twins
¥8,800 up.

❹ Sapporo Washington Hotel (札幌ワシントンホテル)
Kita-Shijo, Nishi 4-chome, Chuo-ku, (011)251-3211. Just beside
Sapporo Station. Singles ¥3,960 up, twins ¥8,800 up.

❺ Yubin Chokin Kaikan (郵便貯金会館)
Minami-Ichiyo, Nishi 26-chome, Chuo-ku (011)642-4321. Three
minutes from Maruyama-koen subway station. Singles ¥3,520,
twins ¥4,620.

SAPPORO EATS & DRINKS

❻ Sapporo Bier Garten
(札幌ビール園 東区北6条東9, Tel. (011)742-1531)
Somebody wisely insisted on not tearing down Sapporo Beer's original brewery. It's been fixed up like a German beer hall inside with
a roaring fire for those cold winter nights, and an outdoor garden
for summer guzzling. Sapporo Beer, Japan's best and the city's
most famous product, never tasted better. On draught, of course.
You can order a variety of snacks such as the island's own potatoes
or corn. The specialty is Genghis Khan barbecue. You grill New
Zealand lamb, plus a variety of vegetables on a gas-fired grill at your
table. Ask for the King Viking special — all the beer you can drink
and Genghis Khan you can eat during a two-hour period, for
¥2,970. If you prefer seafood, always excellent on Hokkaido, ask
for *Dosankoyaki* — salmon, crab and scallops also grilled at the table
(¥1,200). It's wise to make reservations to avoid a possible long
wait. It's a short taxi ride from Sapporo Station. Just tell the driver
"Biiru-en". Free buses leave several times between 6:30-9 p.m. from
the "Garten" to Gobankan Dept., a block from Sapporo Station.
12-9 p.m.

❼ Hyosetsu-no-mon
(氷雪の門 中央区南5条西2, Tel. (011)521-3046)
Hokkaido's own king crab served in 30 different ways is what draws
the crowds to this locally famous place. Entertainment on weekend
evenings.

❽ Ezogoten (えぞ御殿 中央区南3条西6, Tel. (011)241-8051)
More crabs, buttered clams, squid, buttered potatoes served amid
Hokkaido farm implements. 5-11 p.m., closed 1st and 3rd Sun.

❾ Ramen Ryuho
(ラーメン龍鳳 中央区北1条西3, Tel. (011)222-3486)
There are over 300 *ramen* noodle restaurants in this city, but this
one packs them in for its noodles in a brown bean paste sauce (*miso
ramen*). From ¥300. 11 a.m. to 10 p.m., closed Sun.

⑩ Ajino Sampei

(味の三平 中央区南1条西3大丸藤井ビル，Tel.(011)231-0377)

This place claims to have created *miso ramen* way back in 1963. They also started the novelty of adding bean sprouts to the ingredients. 11 a.m. to 7 p.m., closed Mon.

⑪ Sairo (サイロ 中央区南5条西3北専会館，Tel.(011)531-5857)

Ishikari nabe, a winter fish stew made with Hokkaido salmon, is the chief attraction. 5-11 p.m., closed Sun.

⑫ Irohanihoheto

(いろはにほへと 中央区南5条西4，Tel.(011)521-1682)

One of Susukino's most popular drinking spots for young people. Hokkaido snacks with the drinks.

⑬ Tokachi Wine Restaurant (ワインレストラン十勝

南3条西2HBC三条ビル，Tel.(011)221-9085)

Tokachi wine from Hokkaido may be Japan's most famous wine. The Tokachi area's own beef is also served in this basement room which looks like an Italian *trattoria*. 11:30 a.m. to 10 p.m.

⑭ Fransu Ichiba

(仏蘭西市場 中央区南5条西2，Tel.(011)511-0119)

Coffee and antiques, a popular combination in Japan, is what Japanese girls apparently like. Sapporo's young lovelies rate this place high on their list of resting places.

⑮ Ikoi (憩 中央区南5条西5，Tel.(011)521-0918)

Fish nets, pilot wheels, and a buoy or two dispell any doubt about what's offered here — broiled fish from the island's waters. 5:30-12 p.m.

⑯ Restaurant Maison de Savoie

(レストラン・メゾンデサボア 大通西15，Tel.(011)643-5580)

T. Ohara, the owner, offers a tasty ¥1,800 French lunch of several courses, and the vegetables come from his own garden in the country. Warm, homey atmosphere with red brick walls and modern lithographs. 12-2; 5:30-10 p.m., closed Mon. The special lunch is available Tues.-Fri. only.

⑰ Sushi-Dokoro Narita

(鮨処成田 中央区大通西4，Tel.(011)251-8878)

Businessmen and office ladies crowd up to the counter during lunch and dinner hours for the always-fresh and inexpensive *sushi* served here.

SAPPORO SHOPPING

⑱ Seibansha（青盤舎 中央区南7条西4丁目）
The city's best folk craft shop, with lots of Hokkaido's local pottery, plus items from all over Japan. 10 a.m. to 8 p.m., closed Sun.

⑲ Hokkaido Boeki Bussan Shinkokai（北海道貿易物産振興会）
All of the island's famous products on display — Ainu carvings, semi-precious stone jewelry, sealskin accessories, smoked fish, white chocolate and dairy products. Closed Sun.

⑳ Kato Butsusankan（加藤物産館 中央区北4条西4）
One of the city's biggest souvenir shops right in front of Sapporo Station.

㉑ Hokkaido Mingei Center（北海道民芸センター 中央区南2条西6）
More of those gruesome bear carvings, plus a coffee shop in the basement. In Tanukikoji (racoon alley), a covered arcade which draws the city's students.

Clock Tower Building. (Sapporo)

BIBLIOGRAPHY

A History of Japan, by George Sansom, Charles E. Tuttle Co., Inc., Tokyo, 1963. The most readable history of this fascinating country. Comes in a paperback, three-volume set.

Everyday Life in Traditional Japan, by Charles J. Dunn, Charles E. Tuttle Co., Inc., Tokyo, 1969. An interesting look at the lives of the four classes during the Tokugawa era.

The New Official Guide Japan, Japan National Tourist Organization, Japan Travel Bureau, Inc., Tokyo 1975. No sparkling prose, but every detail imaginable. At ¥5,000, only for the very serious.

Kyoto: A Contemplative Guide, by Gouverneur Mosher, Charles E. Tuttle Co., Inc., Tokyo, 1964. Thoughtful musings about Kyoto's best.

Kanazawa: The Other Side of Japan, by Ruth Stevens, Society to Introduce Kanazawa to the World, 1979. A rare thing — details in English on a Japanse provincial city. A must, if you spend any time in Kanazawa.

Touring Tokyo, Junichirō Kuroki and Shinzō Uchida, Kodansha International, Ltd., Tokyo, 1979. A comprehensive look at the urban giant with some handy listings.

Robert's Guide to Japanese Museums, by Laurance P. Roberts, Kodansha International, Ltd., Tokyo, 1978. Practically every museum in Japan is included, with explanations of how to find them.

Foot-loose in Tokyo, by Jean Pearce, Weatherhill, Tokyo, 1976. Walking tours of the neighborhoods around every station on the Yamanote Line which circles Tokyo. Lots of fun.

Eating Cheap in Japan, by Kimiko Nagasawa and Camy Condon, Shufunotomo Co., Ltd., Tokyo, 1972. As essential as your stomach, if you are eating outside the big hotels.

Earth 'n' Fire, by Amaury Saint-Gilles, Shufunotomo Co., Ltd., 1978. Japan's ceramics, kiln by kiln from Kyushu to Hokkaido.

Kites, Crackers and Craftsmen, by Camy Condon and Kimiko Nagasawa, Shufunotomo Co., Ltd., 1974. Listings of 50 shops in Tokyo where things are still made by hand.

What's Japanese about Japan, by John Condon and Keisuke Kurata, Shufunotomo Co., Ltd., Tokyo, 1974. An enlightening attempt to explain the rituals of Japanese life.

Japan: a travel survival kit, by Ian McQueen, Lonely Planet Publications, Victoria, Australia, 1981. Practical information on many out-of-the-way spots.

Sendai, by Margaret Garner, James Vardaman and Ruth Vergin, Keyaki no Machi Co., Ltd., Sendai, 1980. Informative and thorough. Covers the city as well as Matsushima, Hiraizumi and Narugo.

The Narrow Road to the Deep North and Other Travel Sketches, Bashō, translated by Nobuyuki Yuasa, Penguin Books, Harmondsworth, England, 1966. One of those pocket size Penguin Classics.